LEARNING ARABIC WORKBOOK

for Beginners

This book belongs to

Name	Final	Medial	Initial	Isolated	Name in arabic	Page
Alif	ـا	ـا	ا	أ	ألف	4
Bā	ـب	ـبـ	بـ	ب	باء	8
Tā	ـت	ـتـ	تـ	ت	تاء	12
Thā	ـث	ـثـ	ثـ	ث	ثاء	16
Jīm	ـج	ـجـ	جـ	ج	جيم	20
Hā	ـح	ـحـ	حـ	ح	حاء	24
Khā	ـخ	ـخـ	خـ	خ	خاء	28
Dāl	ـد	ـد	د	د	دال	32
Dhāl	ـذ	ـذ	ذ	ذ	ذال	36
Rā	ـر	ـر	ر	ر	راء	40
Zāy	ـز	ـز	ز	ز	زاي	44
Sīn	ـس	ـسـ	سـ	س	سين	48
Shīn	ـش	ـشـ	شـ	ش	شين	52
Sād	ـص	ـصـ	صـ	ص	صاد	56
Dād	ـض	ـضـ	ضـ	ض	ضاد	60
Tā	ـط	ـطـ	طـ	ط	طاء	64
Zhā	ـظ	ـظـ	ظـ	ظ	ظاء	68
Ayn	ـع	ـعـ	عـ	ع	عين	72
Rhayn	ـغ	ـغـ	غـ	غ	غين	76
Fā	ـف	ـفـ	فـ	ف	فاء	80
Qāf	ـق	ـقـ	قـ	ق	قاف	84
Kāf	ـك	ـكـ	كـ	ك	كاف	88
Lām	ـل	ـلـ	لـ	ل	لام	92
Mīm	ـم	ـمـ	مـ	م	ميم	96
Nūn	ـن	ـنـ	نـ	ن	نون	100
Hā	ـه	ـهـ	هـ	ه	هاء	104
Wāw	ـو	ـو	و	و	واو	108
Yā	ـي	ـيـ	يـ	ي	ياء	112
Hamza	ؤ ئ	ـأ ـؤ ـئـ	أ إ	ء	همزة	

Diacritics for Arabic vowels

Fatha ‎ــَ	Damma ‎ــُ	Kasra ‎ــِ
/a/	/o/	/i/
Written above the consonant	Written above the consonant	Written below the consonant
بَ	بُ	بِ
ba	bu	bi

Fatha tanwiin ‎ــً	Damma tanwiin ‎ــٌ	Kasra tanwiin ‎ــٍ
/an/	/on/	/in/
Written above the consonant	Written above the consonant	Written below the consonant
بً	بٌ	بٍ
ban	bun	bin

chadda ‎ــّ	sokoun ‎ــْ
Written above the consonant	Written above the consonant
بّ	بْ
bb	b

ألف   Alif

أَسَدٌ (Lion)

don	sa	a

Final	Medial	Initial
ﻰ	ا	ا

mo-ra-bbaa (Jam)	fa-e-son (Axe)	ar-na-bon (Rabbit)
مُرَبَّى 	فَأْسٌ 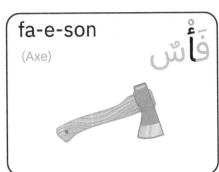	أَرْنَبٌ 

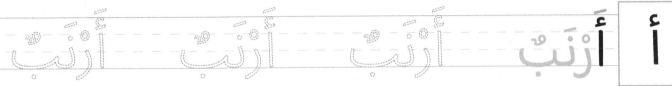

أ	أَرْنَبٌ	أَرْنَبٌ	أَرْنَبٌ	أَرْنَبٌ	أَرْنَبٌ	أَرْنَبٌ

أ	فَأْسٌ	فَأْسٌ	فَأْسٌ	فَأْسٌ	فَأْسٌ	فَأْسٌ

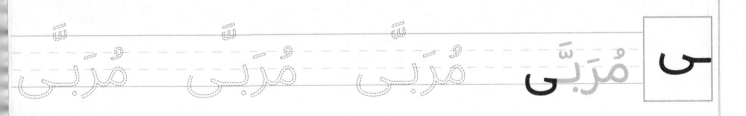

ى	مُرَبَّى	مُرَبَّى	مُرَبَّى	مُرَبَّى	مُرَبَّى	مُرَبَّى

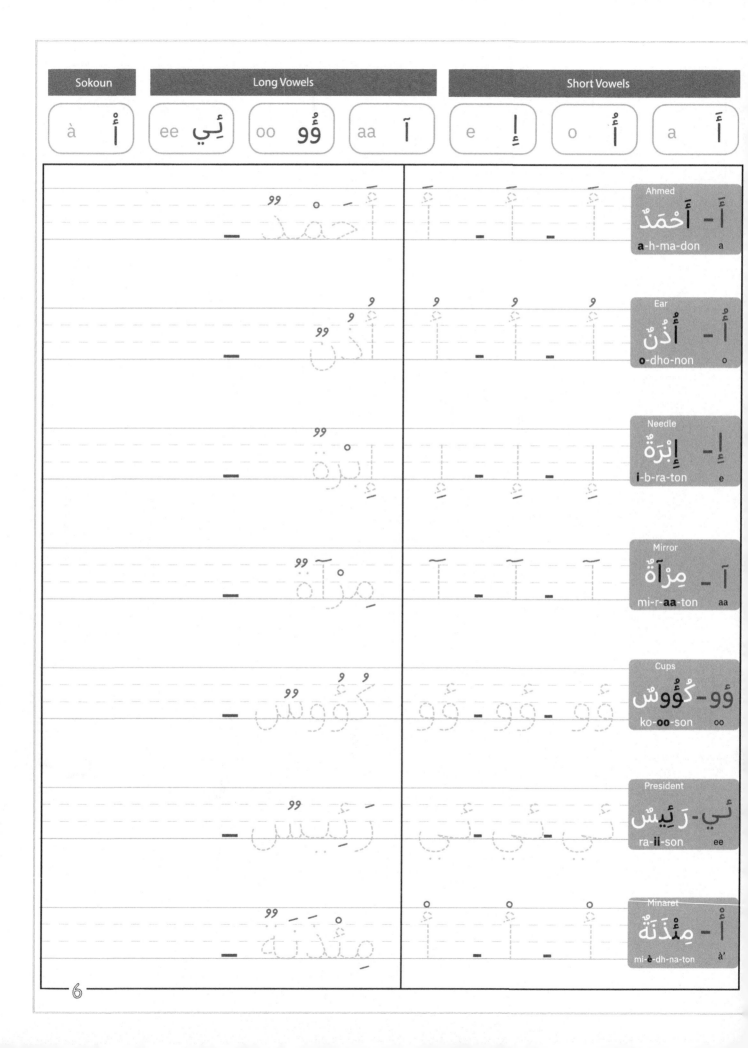

Sokoun	Long Vowels			Short Vowels		
à أْ	ee ئِي	oo وُّ	aa آ	e إِ	o أُ	a أَ

		Ahmed أَ - أَحْمَدٌ a-h-ma-don a
		Ear أُ - أُذُنٌ o-dho-non o
		Needle إِ - إِبْرَةٌ i-b-ra-ton e
		Mirror آ - مِرْآةٌ mi-r-aa-ton aa
		Cups وُّو - كُوُّوسٌ ko-oo-son oo
		President ـِي - رَئِيسٌ ra-ii-son ee
		Minaret أْ - مِئْذَنَةٌ mi-è-dh-na-ton à'

6

Fill in the blank with the correct letter 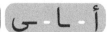 أ - ا - ى

Pear	Book	Teeth

كُمْثَر........	كِتَــَبُ........	........سْنَانُ
ko-ma-th-**aa**	ki-t**aa**-bon	**a**-ss-naa-non

Draw a line to match the words

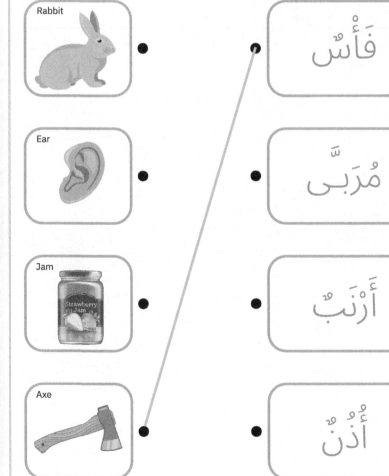

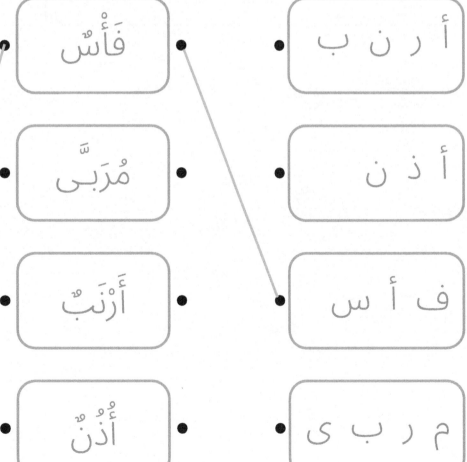

Rabbit

Ear

Jam

Axe

فَأْسٌ

مُرَبَّى

أَرْنَبٌ

أُذْنٌ

أ ر ن ب

أ ذ ن

ف أ س

م ر ب ى

باء **Bā'**

(Parrot) بَبْغَاءٌ

5	4	3	2	1
on	aa	gha	b	ba

Final	Medial	Initial
ـب	ـبـ	بـ

qa-l-bon (Heart)  قَلْبٌ	hi-b-ron (Ink) 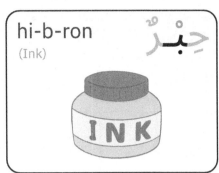 حِبْرٌ	ba-qa-ra-ton (Cow)  بَقَرَةٌ

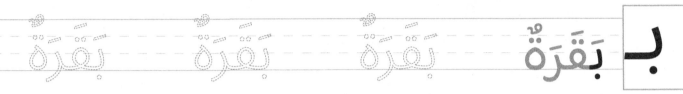

ب بَقَرَةٌ

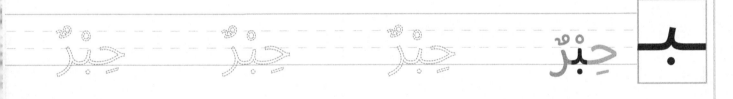

ب حِبْرٌ

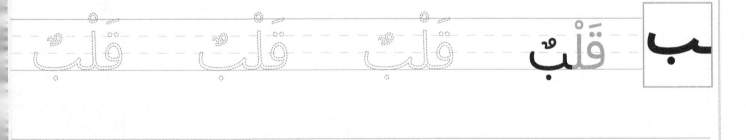

ب قَلْبٌ

| ب b' | بي bee | بو boo | با baa | بِ be | بُ bo | بَ ba |

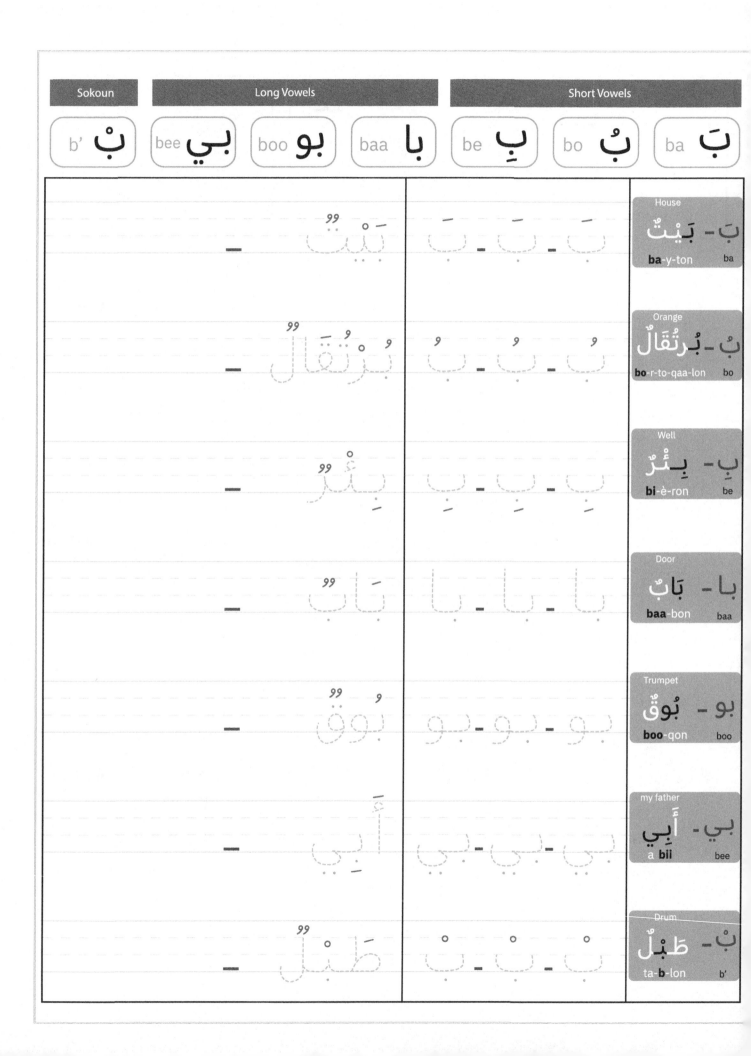

House
بَ - بَيْتٌ
ba-y-ton — ba

Orange
بُ - بُرْتُقَالٌ
bo-r-to-qaa-lon — bo

Well
بِ - بِئْرٌ
bi-è-ron — be

Door
با - بَابٌ
baa-bon — baa

Trumpet
بو - بُوقٌ
boo-qon — boo

my father
بي - أَبِي
a bii — bee

Drum
بْ - طَبْلٌ
ta-b-lon — b'

Fill in the blank with the correct letter

Dog	Suitcase	Duck

كَلًّ.......	حَقِيـ.......ـةً	.......ـطَّةً
ka-l-**bon**	ha-qii-**ba**-ton	**ba**-tta-ton

Draw a line to match the words

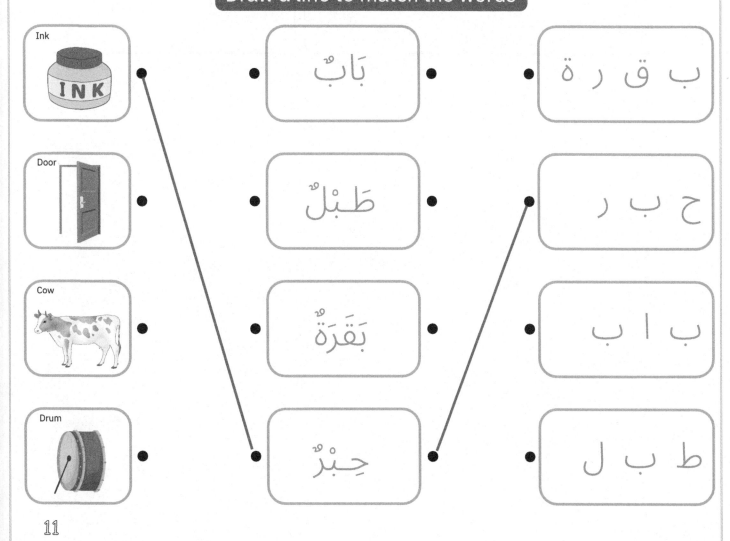

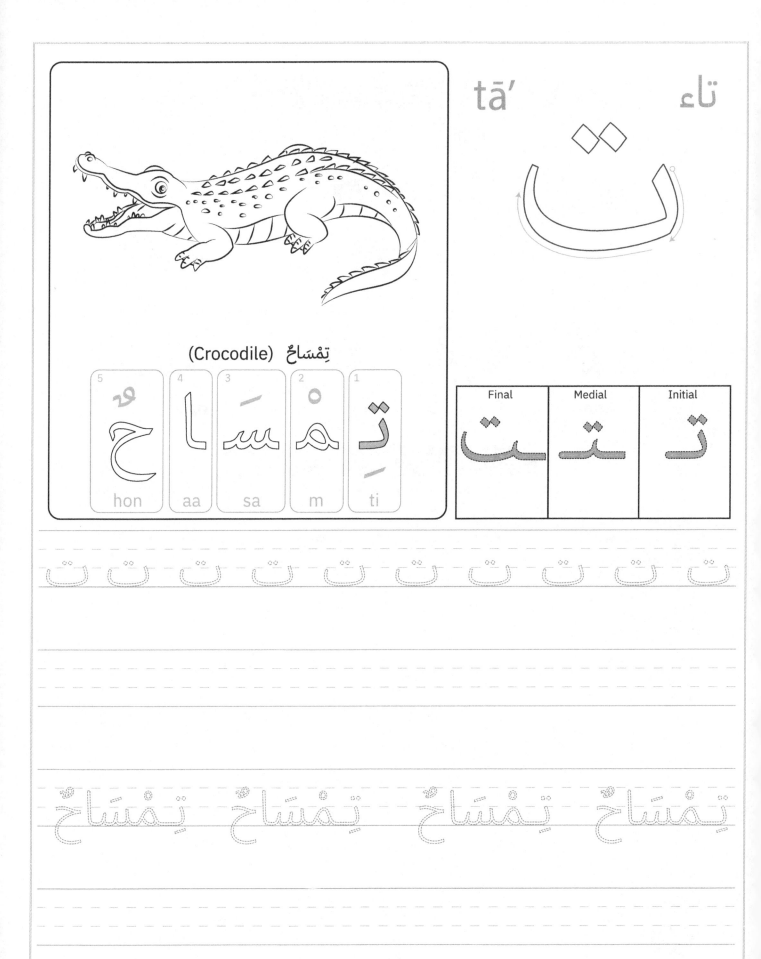

تاء tā'

(Crocodile) تِمْسَاحٌ

5 وو	4 ــ	3 ــ	2 ه	1 ــ
hon	aa	sa	m	ti

Final	Medial	Initial
ت	ـتـ	تـ

ba-y-ton
(House)

بَيْت

ma-t-ha-fon
(Museum)

مَتْحَف

to-ffaa-hon
(Apple)

تُفَاح

ت | تُفَاح

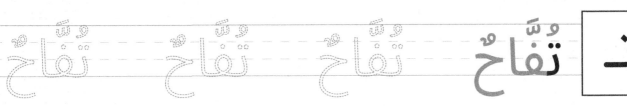

ت | مَتْحَف

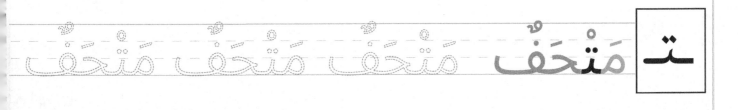

ت | بَيْت

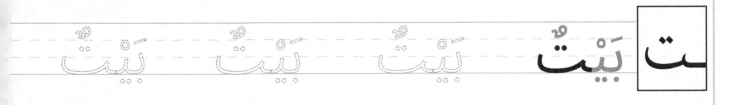

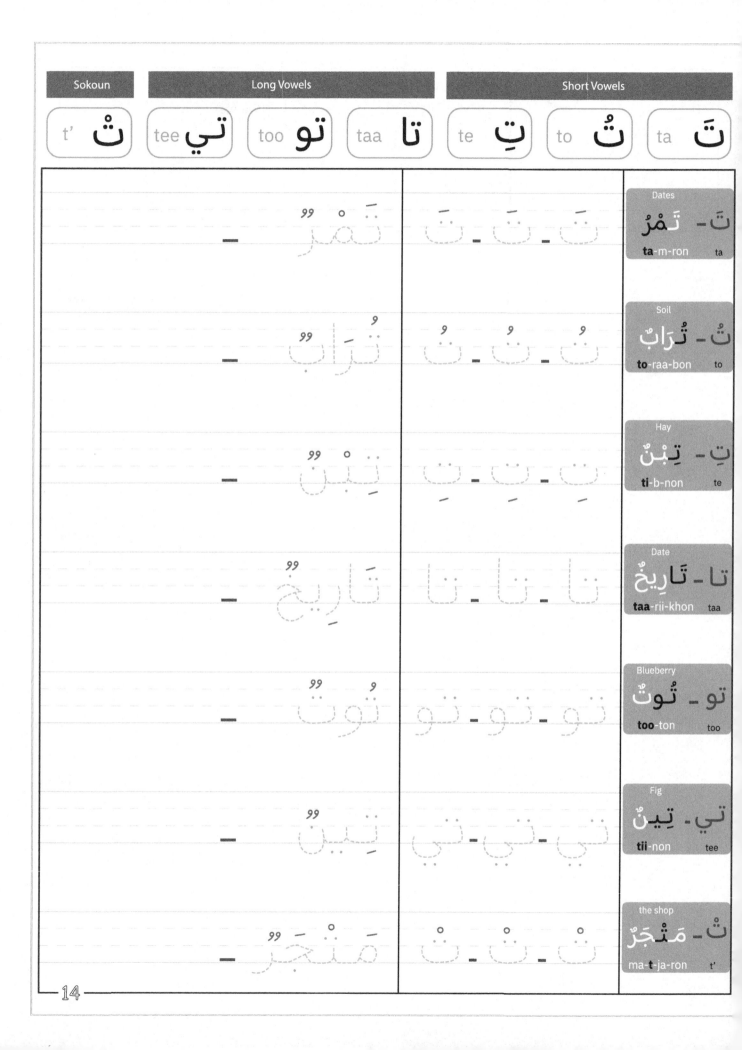

Sokoun	Long Vowels			Short Vowels		
ثْ t'	تِي tee	تُو too	تَا taa	تِ te	تُ to	تَ ta

Dates ت - تَمْرُ **ta**-m-ron	ta
Soil ثُ - تُرَابٌ **to**-raa-bon	to
Hay تِ - تِبْنٌ **ti**-b-non	te
Date تَا - تَارِيخٌ **taa**-rii-khon	taa
Blueberry تُو - تُوتٌ **too**-ton	too
Fig تِي - تِينٌ **tii**-non	tee
the shop ثْ - مَتْجَرٌ **ma-t**-ja-ron	t'

14

Girl	Notebook	Crown

بِنْ	دِفْرُ	ـاجُ
bi-n-**ton**	di-f-**ta**-ron	**taa**-jon

Draw a line to match the words

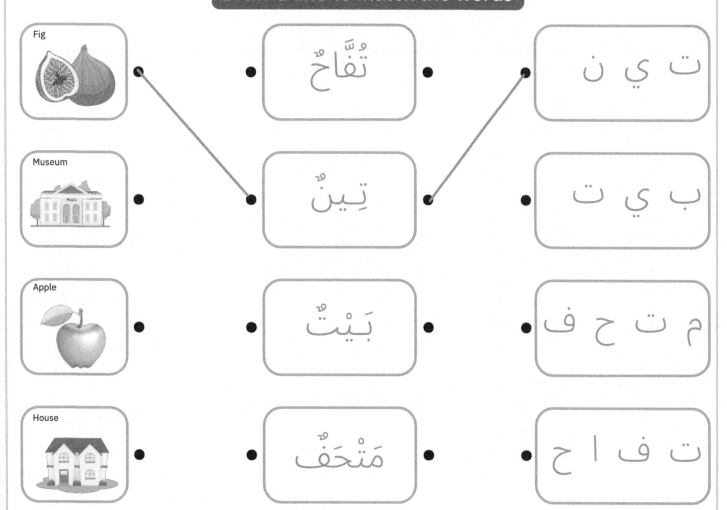

Fig	تُفَّاحُ	ت ي ن
Museum	تِينْ	ب ي ت
Apple	بَيْتْ	م ت ح ف
House	مَتْحَفُ	ت ف ا ج

thā   ثاء

ثَعْلَبٌ (Fox)

4	3	2	1
بْ	لَ	عَ	ثَ
bon	la	â	tha

Final	Medial	Initial
ث	ث	ث

16

mo-tha-lla-thon (Triangle) مُثَلَّث	thi-m-thaa-lon (Statue) تِمْثَال	tha-w-ron (Oxe) ثَوْر

| ثَوْر | ثَوْر | ثَوْر | ثَوْر | ثَوْر | ذ ثَوْر ث |

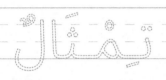

| تِمْثَال | تِمْثَال | تِمْثَال | تِمْثَال | ثـ ثّ |

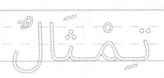

| مُثَلَّث | مُثَلَّث | مُثَلَّث | مُثَلَّث | ث مُثَلَّث |

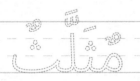
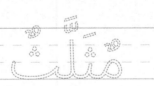

17

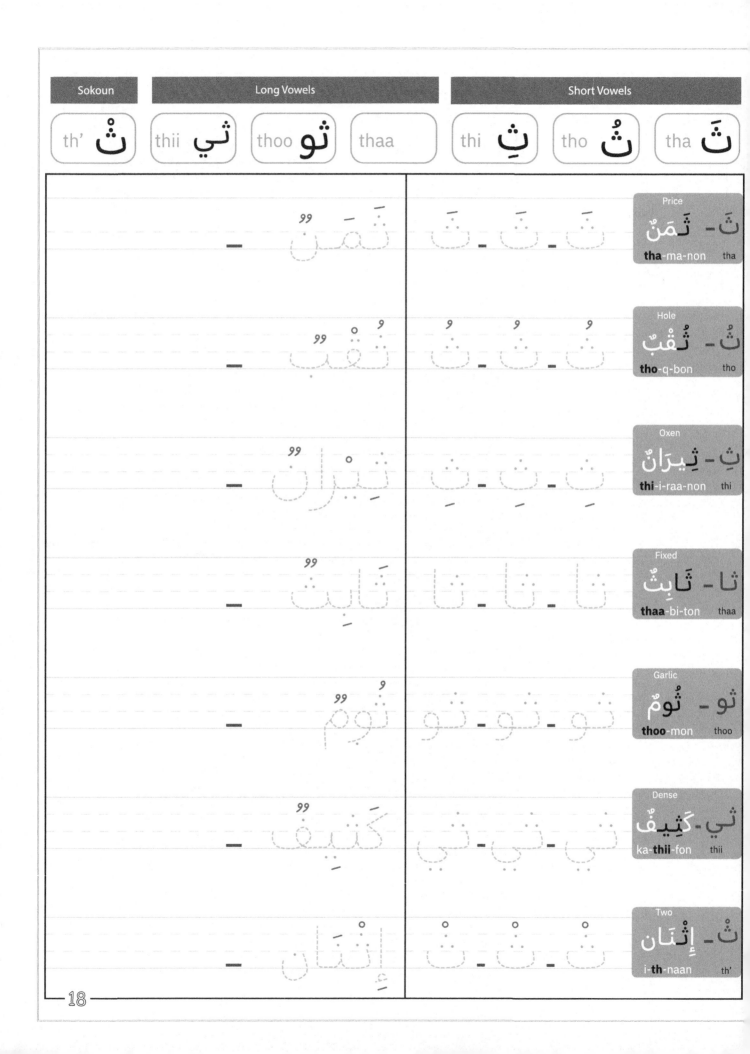

Price
ثَ - ثَمَنٌ
tha-ma-non   tha

Hole
ثُ - ثُقْبٌ
tho-q-bon   tho

Oxen
ثِ - ثِيرَانٌ
thi-i-raa-non   thi

Fixed
ثَا - ثَابِتٌ
thaa-bi-ton   thaa

Garlic
ثُو - ثُومٌ
thoo-mon   thoo

Dense
ثِي - كَثِيفٌ
ka-**thii**-fon   thii

Two
ثْ - إِثْنَان
i-**th**-naan   th'

Plow

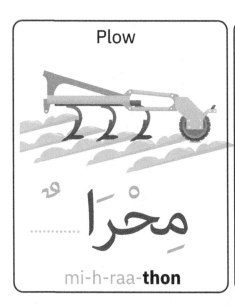

مِحْرَا.........

mi-h-raa-**thon**

Triangle

مُـ.........ـلَّثُ

mo-**tha**-lla-thon

Snake

.........ُعْبَانٌ

tho-â-baa-non

Draw a line to match the words

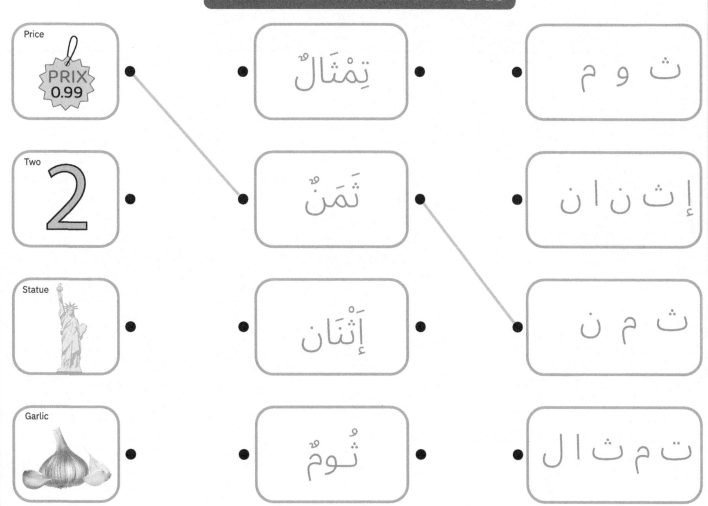

Price
PRIX
0.99

Two
2

Statue

Garlic

تِمْثَالٌ

ثَمَنٌ

إَثْنَان

ثُومٌ

ث و م

إ ث ن ا ن

ث م ن

ت م ث ا ل

19

Jīm

جِيم

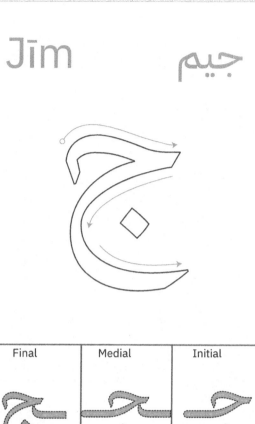

(Camel) جَمَلٌ

3	2	1
لُ	مَ	جَ
lon	ma	ja

Final	Medial	Initial
ج	ـجـ	جـ

ج ج ج ج ج ج ج ج ج ج ج ج

جَمَلٌ جَمَلٌ جَمَلٌ جَمَلٌ جَمَلٌ

20

tha-l-jon
(Snow)

ثَلْج

ma-ja-rra-ton
(Galaxy)

مَجَرَّة

ja-r-won
(Puppy)

جَرْوٌ

جَرْوٌ | جَرْوٌ | جَرْوٌ | جَرْوٌ جـ

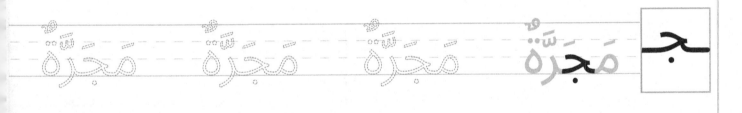

مَجَرَّة | مَجَرَّة | مَجَرَّة | مَجَرَّة ـجـ

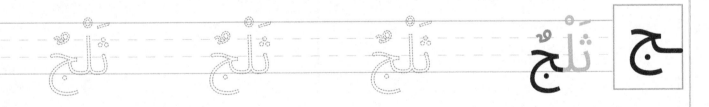

ثَلْجُ | ثَلْجُ | ثَلْجُ | ثَلْجُ ـج

21

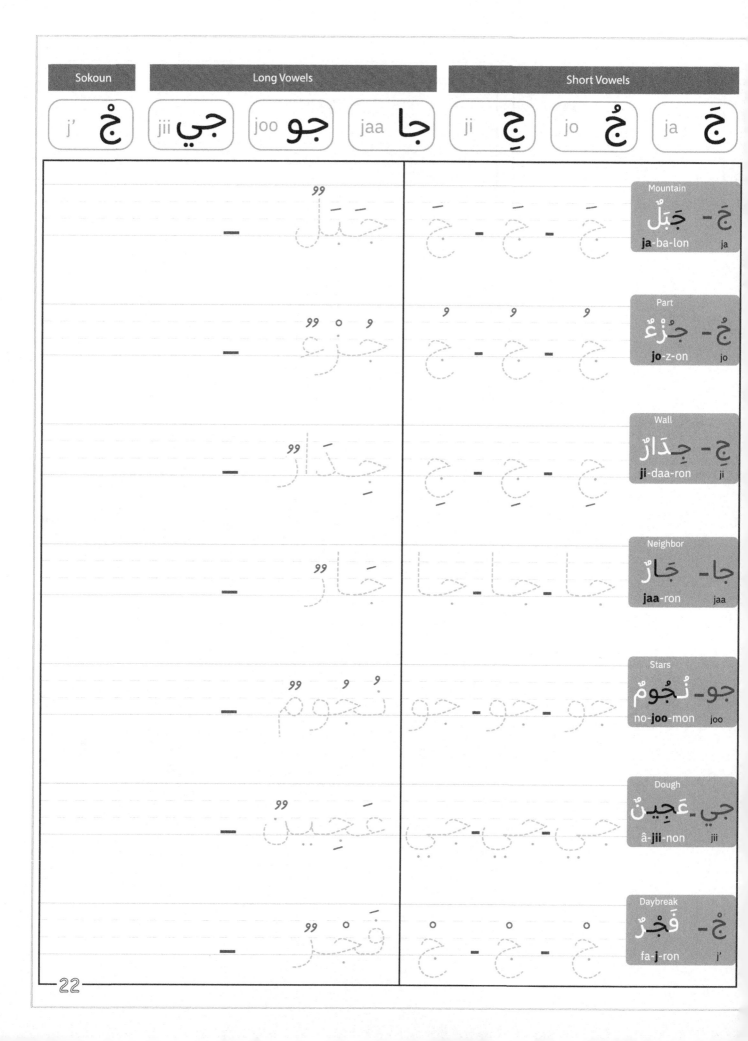

Stairs	Cup	Cheese

دَرْ......ُ	فِنْ......َانُ	......ْبْنُ
da-r-**jon**	fin-**jaa**-non	**jo**-b-non

Draw a line to match the words

Puppy

ثَلْجُ

ن ج و م

Snow

نُجُومُ

ث ل ج

Mountain

جَرْوُ

ج ب ل

Stars

جَبَلُ

ج ر و

23

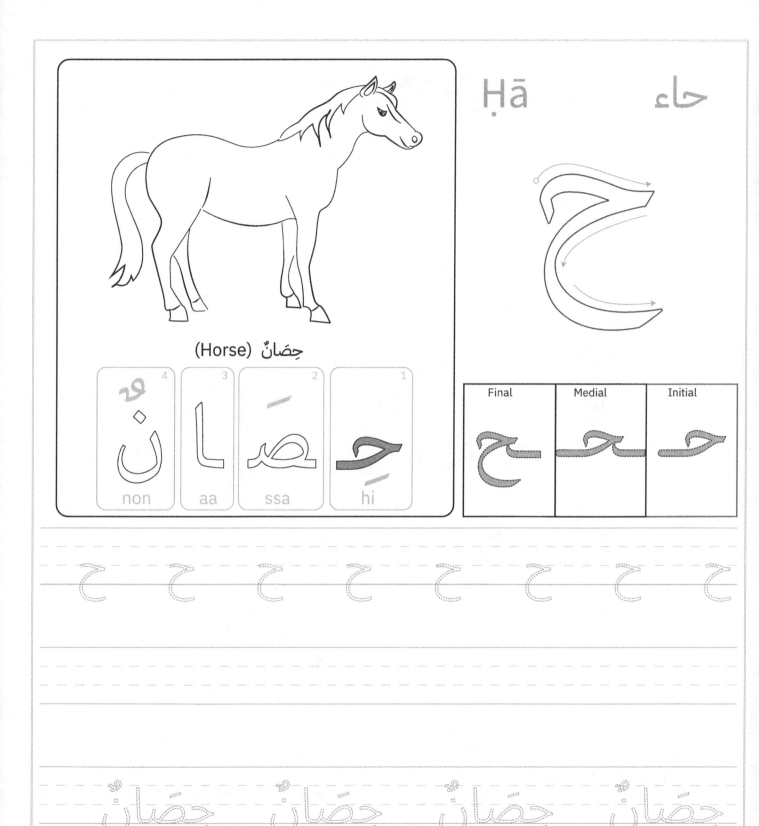

Ḥā

حاء

جِصَانٌ (Horse)

4	3	2	1
نْ	ـان	ـصَ	حِ
non	aa	ssa	hi

Final	Medial	Initial
ـح	ـحـ	حـ

ح ح ح ح ح ح ح ح

جِصَانٌ   جِصَانٌ   جِصَانٌ   جِصَانٌ

ma-ss-ba-hon	مَسْبَح	ba-h-ron	بَحْرٌ	hi-maa-ron	حِمَارٌ
(swimming pool)		(Sea)		(Donkey)	

حِمَارٌ حِمَارٌ حِمَارٌ ح حِ

بَحْرٌ بَحْرٌ بَحْرٌ ح

مَسْبَح مَسْبَح مَسْبَح ح

		Garden
خَ - حَدِيقَةٌ	ha-dii-qa-ton	ha

		Cereal
خُ - حُبُوبٌ	ho-boo-bon	ho

		Shoe
حِ - حِذَاءٌ	hi-dhaa-on	hi

		Bus
حَا - حَافِلَةٌ	haa-fi-la-ton	haa

		Suhoor
حُو - سُحُورٌ	so-hoo-ron	hoo

		Whales
حِي - حِيتَانٌ	hii-taa-non	hii

		Sea
خْ - بَحْرٌ	ba-h-ron	h'

Sel	Viande	Lait

مِلْـ‍ُ	لَـ‍ْم	‍ِليبٌ
mi-l-**hon**	la-**h**-mon	**ha**-lii-bon

Draw a line to match the words

Bus

مَسْبَحٌ

ح م ا ر

Donkey

حَافِلَةٌ

ح ا ف ل ة

Sea

حِذَاءٌ

ح ذ ا ء

Shoe

حِمَارٌ

م س ب ح

Khā خاء

(Sheep) خَرُوفٌ

4	3	2	1
ف	و	ر	خ
fon	oo	ro	kha

Final	Medial	Initial
خ	خ	خ

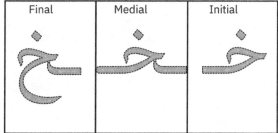

ح ح ح ح ح ح ح ح

خَرُوفٌ خَرُوفٌ خَرُوفٌ خَرُوفٌ

ba-ttii-khon (Watermelon) بَطِّيخ	sa-kh-ra-ton (a rock) صَخْرَة	kha-sson (Lettuce) خَسٌّ

خَـ | خَسٌّ

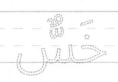 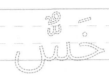 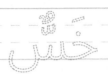

خـ | صَخْرَة

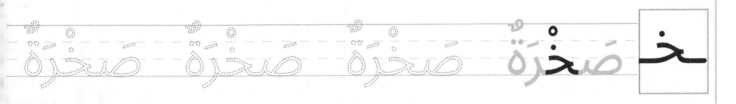

خ | بَطِّيخ

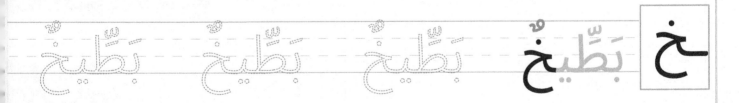

| خْ kh' | خِي khii | خُو khoo | خَا khaa | خِ khi | خُ kho | خَ kha |

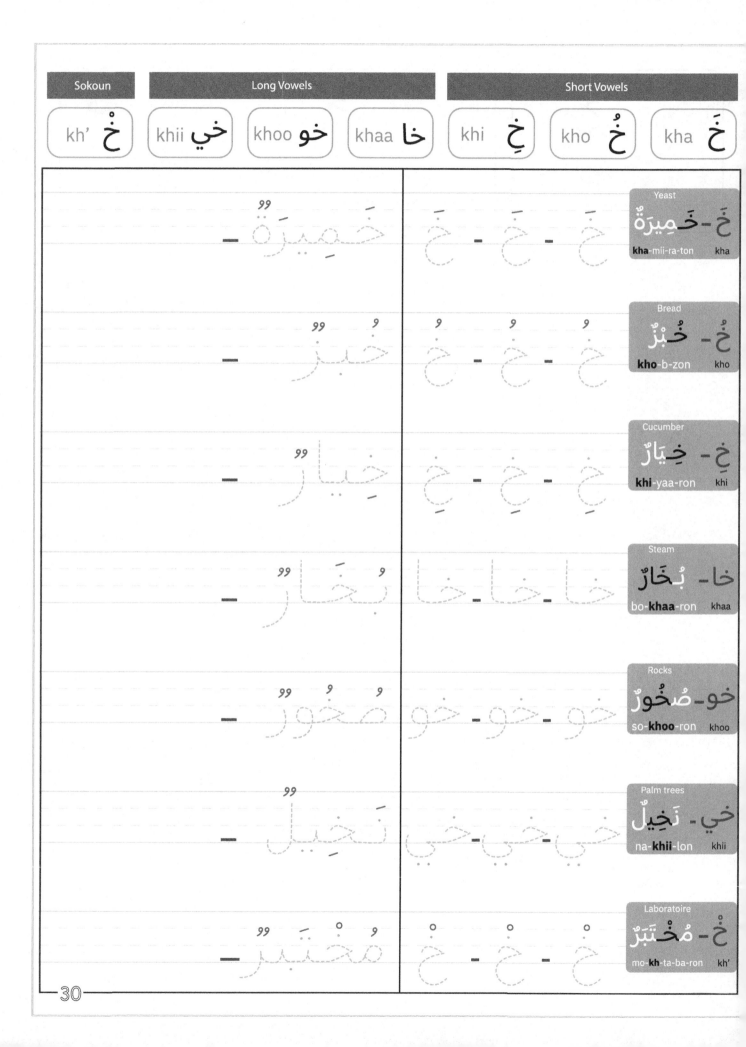

Yeast
خَمِيرَةٌ - خَ
kha-mii-ra-ton   kha

Bread
خُبْزٌ - خُ
kho-b-zon   kho

Cucumber
خِيَارٌ - خِ
khi-yaa-ron   khi

Steam
بُخَارٌ - خَا
bo-**khaa**-ron   khaa

Rocks
صُخُورٌ - خُو
so-**khoo**-ron   khoo

Palm trees
نَخِيلٌ - خِي
na-**khii**-lon   khii

Laboratoire
مُخْتَبَرٌ - خْ
mo-**kh**-ta-ba-ron   kh'

30

Fill in the blank with the correct letter

Peach	Palm	Wood

ـــخُو	نَـــْلَةٌ	ـَشَبٌ
khoo-**khon**	na-**kh**-la-ton	**kha**-sha-bon

Draw a line to match the words

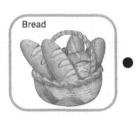 Bread

 خ س

خِيَارٌ

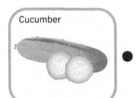 Cucumber

ب ط ي خ

بَطِّيخٌ

 Watermelon

خ ي ا ر

خُبْزٌ

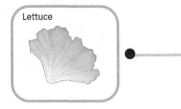 Lettuce

خ ب ز

خَسٌّ

31

Dāl   دال

دَرَّاجَةٌ (Bicycle)

5	4	3	2	1
ةُ	ـجَ	ا	رَّ	دَ
ton	ja	aa	rr	da

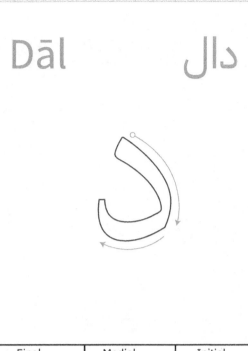

Final	Medial	Initial
ـد	ـد	د

دَرَّاجَةٌ   دَرَّاجَةٌ   دَرَّاجَةٌ   دَرَّاجَةٌ

32

mass-ji-don
(Mosque)
مَسْجِدٌ

ma-d-ra-sa-ton
(School)
مَدْرَسَةٌ

do-l-fii-non
(Dolphin)
دُلْفِينٌ

د دُلْفِينٌ دُلْفِينٌ دُلْفِينٌ

دـ مَدْرَسَةٌ مَدْرَسَةٌ مَدْرَسَةٌ

ـد مَسْجِدٌ مَسْجِدٌ مَسْجِدٌ

| ذْ d' | دِي dii | دو doo | دا daa | دِ di | دُ do | دَ da |

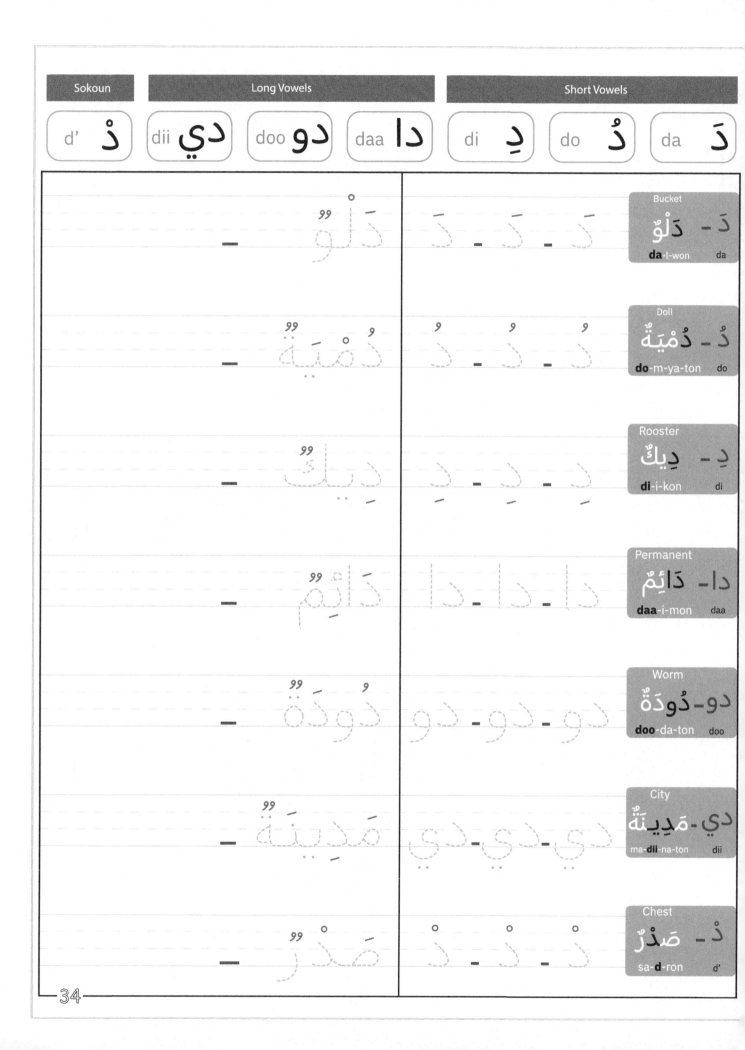

Bucket

دَ - دَلْوٌ

da-l-won   da

Doll

دُ - دُمْيَةٌ

do-m-ya-ton   do

Rooster

دِ - دِيكٌ

di-i-kon   di

Permanent

دا- دَائِمٌ

daa-i-mon   daa

Worm

دو-دُودَةٌ

doo-da-ton   doo

City

دي -مَدِينَةٌ

ma-dii-na-ton   dii

Chest

ذْ - صَدْرٌ

sa-d-ron   d'

Monkey	Box	Bear

‎قِرْ......دٌ‎	‎صُنْ......وقٌ‎	‎......بٌّ‎
qi-r--**don**	so-n-**doo**-qon	**do**-bbon

Draw a line to match the words

Rooster 	‎دِيكٌ‎	‎د ل و‎
Bucket	‎دُلْفِينٌ‎	‎م د ر س ة‎
School 	‎دَلْوٌ‎	‎د ي ك‎
Dolphin 	‎مَدْرَسَةٌ‎	‎د ل ف ي ن‎

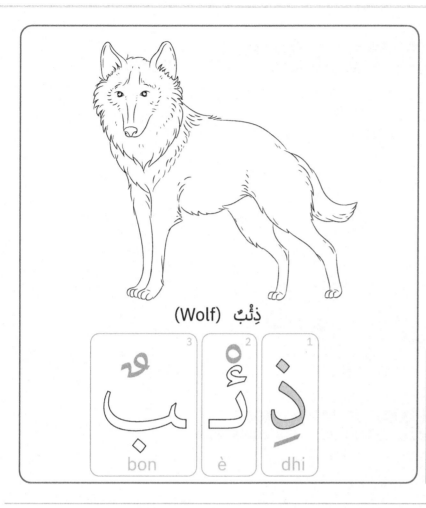

ذِئْبٌ (Wolf)

3	2	1
ب	ئـ	ذ
bon	è	dhi

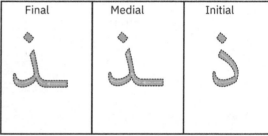

Final	Medial	Initial
ـذ	ـذـ	ذ

ذ ذ ذ ذ ذ ذ ذ ذ ذ ذ

ذِئْبْ ذِئْبْ ذِئْبْ ذِئْبْ ذِئْبْ ذِئْبْ ذِئْبْ ذِئْبْ

ti-ll-mii-dhon	o-dho-non	dho-ra-ton
(Pupil) تِلْمِيذٌ	(Ear) أُذُنٌ	(Maize) ذُرَةٌ

 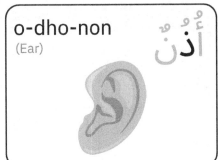 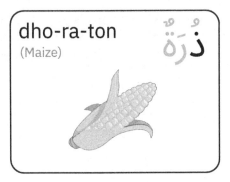

ذُرَةٌ ذ

أُذُنٌ ـذ

تِلْمِيذٌ ـذ

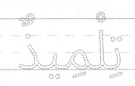 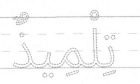 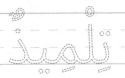 

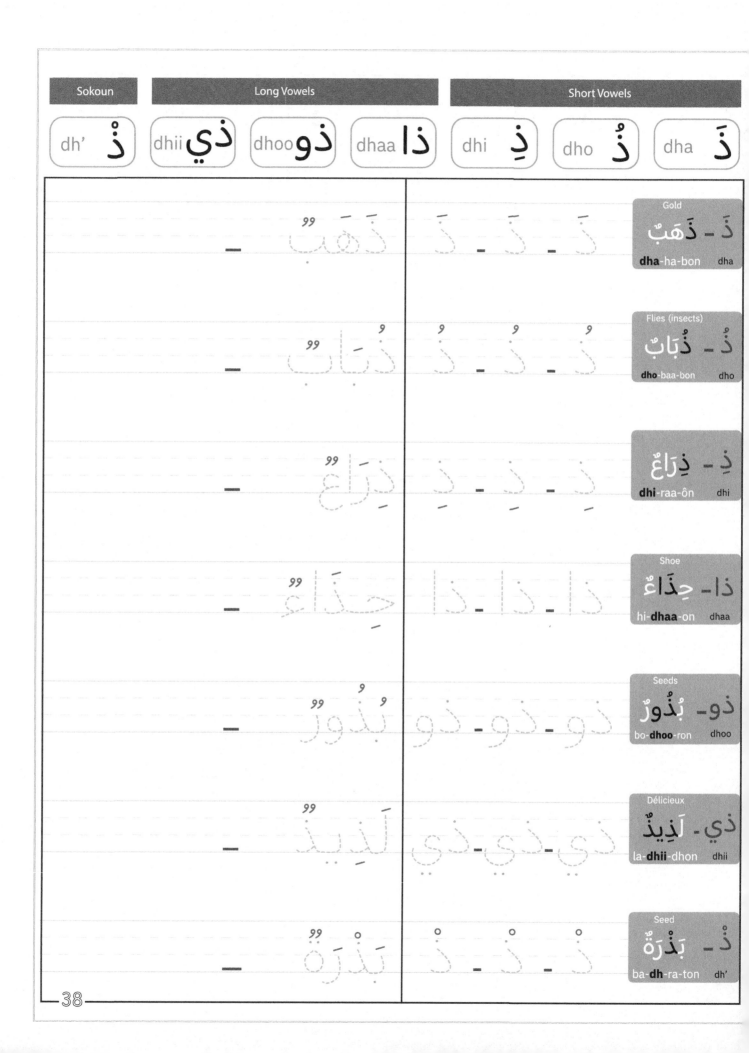

Gold
ذَ - ذَهَبٌ
dha-ha-bon   dha

Flies (insects)
ذُ - ذُبَابٌ
dho-baa-bon   dho

ذِ - ذِرَاعٌ
dhi-raa-ôn   dhi

Shoe
ذا - حِذَاءٌ
hi-dhaa-on   dhaa

Seeds
ذو - بُذُورٌ
bo-dhoo-ron   dhoo

Délicieux
ذي - لَذِيذٌ
la-dhii-dhon   dhii

Seed
ذْ - بَذْرَةٌ
ba-dh-ra-ton   dh'

Fill in the blank with the correct letter ذ ـ ـذ

hedgehog	shoes	Tail

قُنْفُ........	حِ........ـاءٌ	........ـيْلٌ
qo-n-fo-**dhon**	hi-**dhaa**-on	**dha**-y-lon

Draw a line to match the words

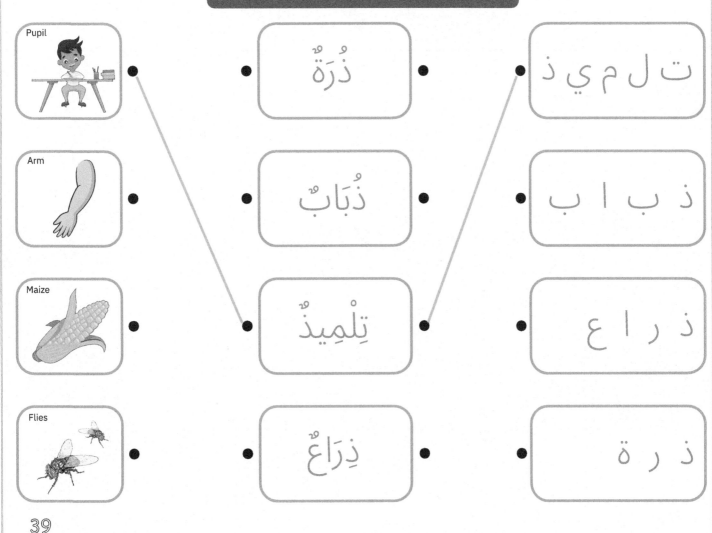

Pupil

Arm

Maize

Flies

ذُرَةٌ

ذُبَابٌ

تِلْمِيذٌ

ذِرَاعٌ

ت ل م ي ذ

ذ ب ا ب

ذ ر ا ع

ذ ر ة

Rā راء

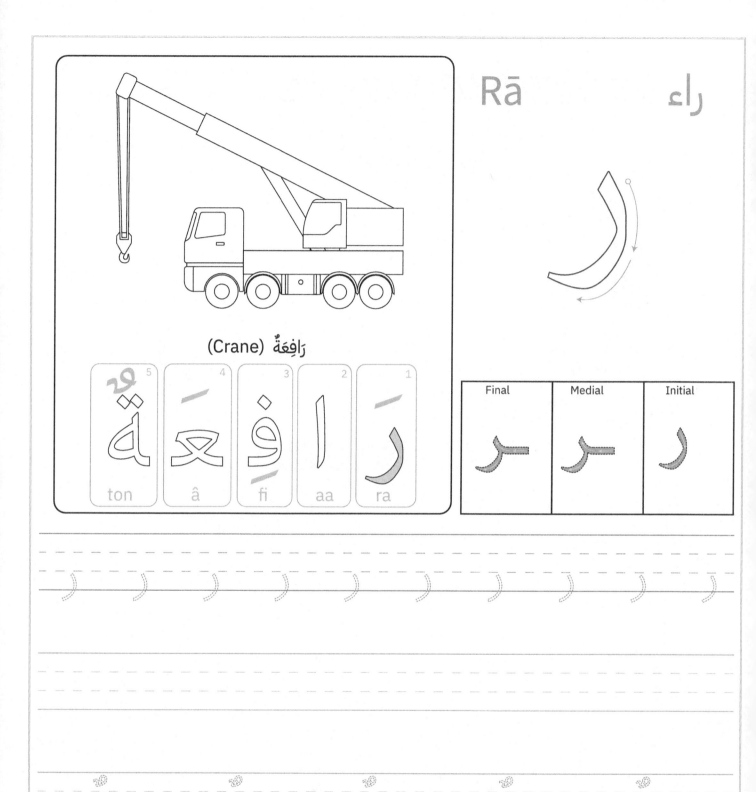

رَافِعَةٌ (Crane)

5	4	3	2	1
ون ة	عِ	فِ	ا	رَ
ton	â	fi	aa	ra

Final	Medial	Initial
ـر	ـرـ	ر

na-hh-ron	dhi-raa-ôn	ra-è-son
(River) نَهْرٌ	(Arm) ذِرَاعٌ	(Head) رَأْسٌ

  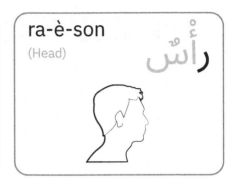

ر	رَأْسٌ	رَأْسٌ رَأْسٌ	رَأْسٌ رَأْسٌ	رَأْسٌ رَأْسٌ

ـر	ذِرَاعٌ	ذِرَاعٌ ذِرَاعٌ	ذِرَاعٌ ذِرَاعٌ	ذِرَاعٌ ذِرَاعٌ

ـر	نَهْرٌ	نَهْرٌ نَهْرٌ	نَهْرٌ نَهْرٌ	نَهْرٌ نَهْرٌ

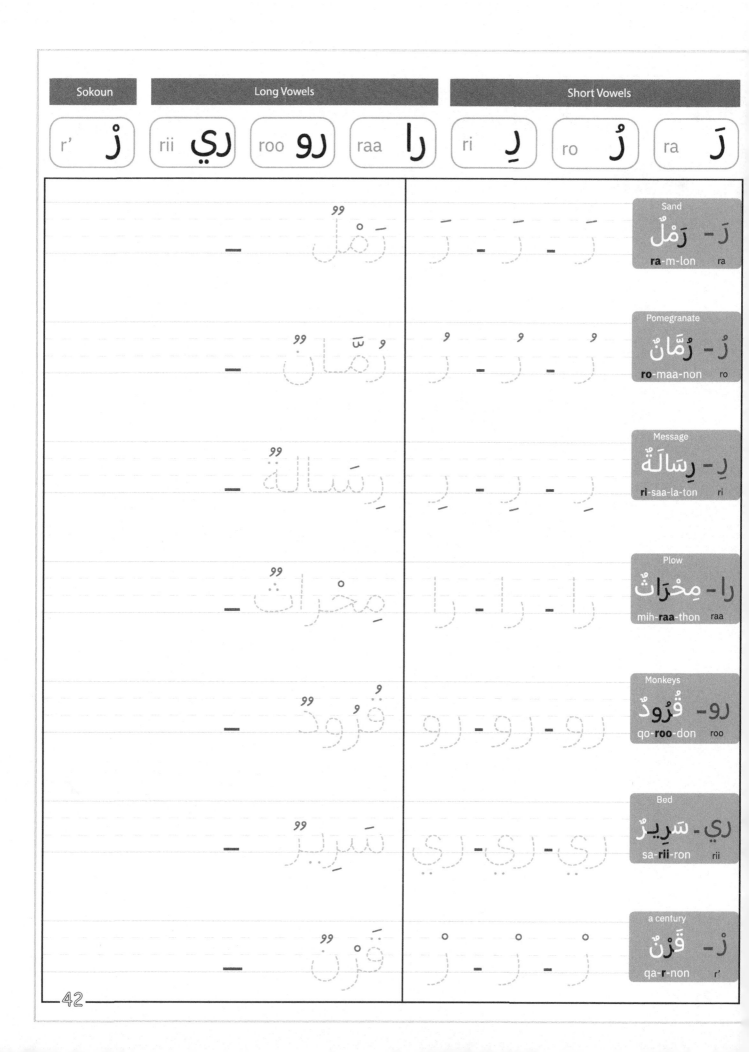

Short Vowels
Sand رَ- رَمْلٌ **ra**-m-lon ra
Pomegranate رُ- رُمَّانٌ **ro**-maa-non ro
Message رِ- رِسَالَةٌ **ri**-saa-la-ton ri
Plow را- مِحْرَاثٌ mih-**raa**-thon raa
Monkeys رو- قُرُودٌ qo-**roo**-don roo
Bed رِي- سَرِيرٌ sa-**rii**-ron rii
a century رْ- قَرْنٌ qa-**r**-non r'

Bridge	Tree	Raccoon

جِسْـــــ	شَـجَــــةٌ	ـــاكُونُ
ji-ss-**ron**	cha-ja-**ra**-ton	**raa**-koo-non

Draw a line to match the words

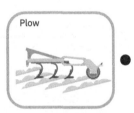 Plow

رُمَّانٌ

س ر ي ر

 Bed

نَهْرٌ

م ح ر ا ث

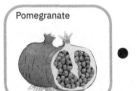 Pomegranate

مِحْرَاثٌ

ن ه ر

 River

سَرِيرٌ

ر م ا ن

Zāy   زاي

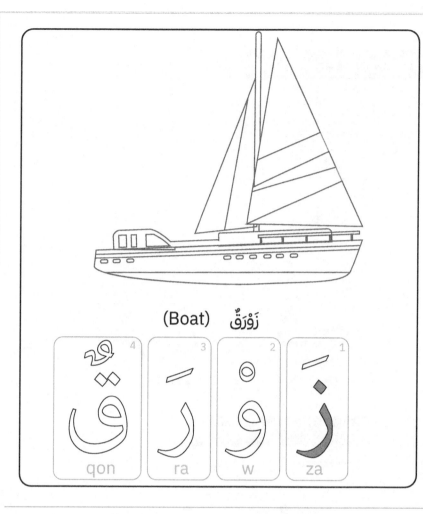

(Boat) زَوْرَقٌ

4	3	2	1
قۏ	رَ	وْ	زَ
qon	ra	w	za

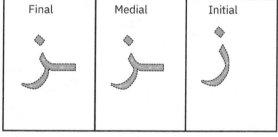

Final	Medial	Initial
ـز	ـزـ	ز

ka-ra-zon
(Cherry)
كَرَزْ

ja-zii-ra-ton
(Island)
جَزِيرَةٌ

za-raa-fa-ton
(Giraffe)
زَرَافَةٌ

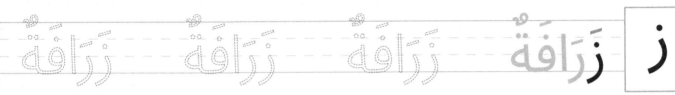

زَرَافَةٌ | ز

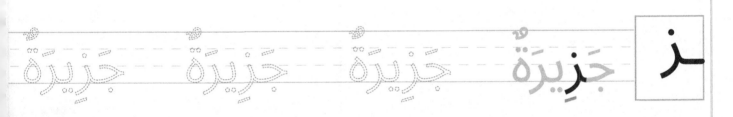

جَزِيرَةٌ | ـز

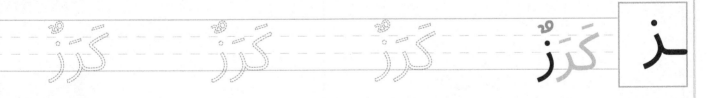

كَرَزْ | ـز

a flower
زَ- زَهْرَةٌ
za-h-ra-ton za

Butter
زُ- زُبْدَةٌ
zo-b-da-ton zo

Button
زِ- زِرٌّ
zi-rron zi

An angle
زا- زَاوِيَةٌ
zaa-wi-ya-ton zaa

Snail
زو- حَلَزُونٌ
ha-la-zoo-non zoo

Determination
زِي - عَزِيمَةٌ
â-zii-ma-ton zii

Farm
زْ- مَزْرَعَةٌ
ma-z-ra-âa-ton z'

Glove	House	Flowers

قُفَاّ ـ	مَنْـِلُ	ـهورُ
qo-ffaa-**zon**	ma-n-**zi**-lon	**zo**-hoo-ron

Draw a line to match the words

Snail 	زَهْرَةٌ	ح ل ز و ن
Flowers	حَلَزُونٌ	ز ه ر ة
Island	كَرَزٌ	ج ز ي ر ة
Cherry	جَزِيرَةٌ	ك ر ز

سَيَّارَةٌ (Car)

5	4	3	2	1
ۃ	رَ	ا	يَّ	سَ
ton	ra	aa	yya	sa

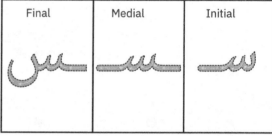

Final	Medial	Initial
ـس	ـسـ	سـ

س س س س س س س

سَيَّارَةٌ سَيَّارَةٌ سَيَّارَةٌ سَيَّارَةٌ سَيَّارَةٌ

ja-ra-son
(Bell)

جَرَسٌ

ma-ss-ra-hon
(Theater)

مَسْرَحٌ

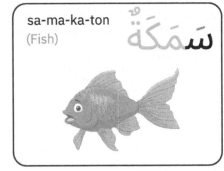

sa-ma-ka-ton
(Fish)

سَمَكَةٌ

سَمَكَةٌ 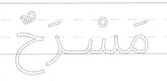	سَمَكَةٌ 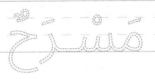	سَمَكَةٌ 	سَ	سـ

مَسْرَحٌ 	مَسْرَحٌ 	مَسْرَحٌ 	مَسْ	سـ

جَرَسٌ	جَرَسٌ	جَرَسٌ	جَرَسٌ	س

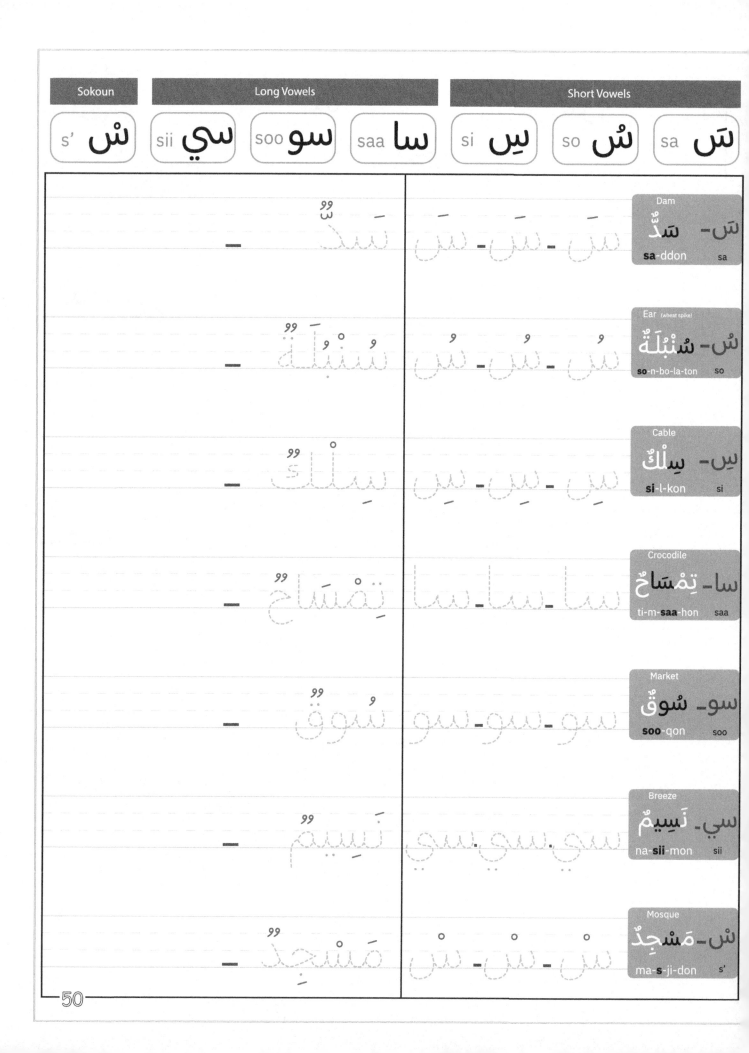

		Dam
		سَدٌّ -سَ
		sa-ddon · sa

		Ear (wheat spike)
		سُنْبُلَةٌ -سُ
		so-n-bo-la-ton · so

		Cable
		سِلْكٌ -سِ
		si-l-kon · si

		Crocodile
		تِمْسَاحٌ -سَا
		ti-m-**saa**-hon · saa

		Market
		سُوقٌ -سُو
		soo-qon · soo

		Breeze
		نَسِيمٌ -سِي
		na-**sii**-mon · sii

		Mosque
		مَسْجِدٌ -سْ
		ma-**s**-ji-don · s'

Pineapple	Honey	Squirrel

أَنَانَا	عَ .... لُ	.... نْجَابٌ
a-na-na-**s**	âa-**sa**-lon	**si**-n-jaa-bon

Draw a line to match the words

Fish 	تِمْسَاحٌ	س م ك ة
Bell	سِنْبُلَةٌ	ت م س ا ح
Ear 	جَرَسٌ	س ن ب ل ة
Crocodile 	سَمَكَةٌ	ج ر س

51

Sheen شين

شَجَرَةٌ (Tree)

4 ةٌ	3 رَ	2 جَ	1 شَ
ton	ra	ja	sha

Final	Medial	Initial
ش	ـشـ	شـ

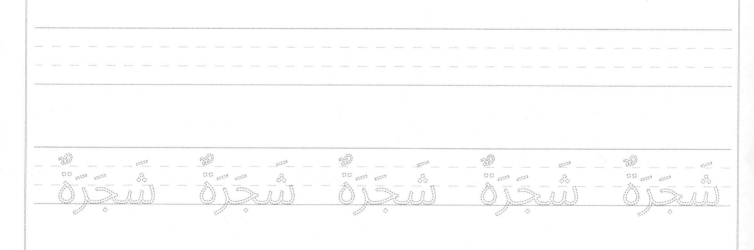

ش ش ش ش ش ش ش ش

شَجَرَة شَجَرَة شَجَرَة شَجَرَة شَجَرَة

| ö-sh'sh-on
(Nest) | عُش | mo-sh-ton
(Comb) | مُشط | sha-â-ron
(Hair) | شَعْر |

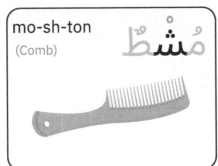

| شَعْر | شَعْر | شَعْر | شَعْر | شَعْر | شَعْر | شَعْر | شَـ |

| مُشط | مُشط | مُشط | مُشط | مُشط | مُشط | مُشط | شـ |

| عُش | عُش | عُش | عُش | عُش | عُش | عُش | شـ |

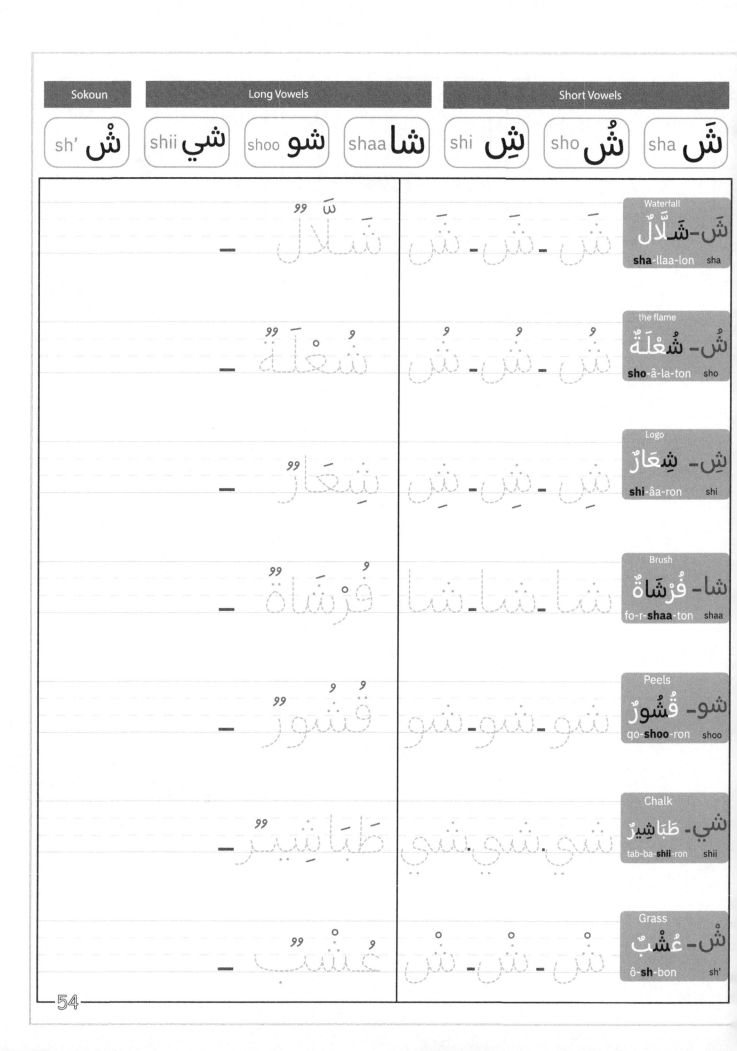

Waterfall
شَ-شَلَّالٌ
sha-llaa-ton   sha

the flame
شُ-شُعْلَةٌ
sho-â-la-ton   sho

Logo
شِ-شِعَارٌ
shi-âa-ron   shi

Brush
شا-فُرْشَاةٌ
fo-r-shaa-ton   shaa

Peels
شو-قُشُورٌ
qo-shoo-ron   shoo

Chalk
شي-طَبَاشِيرٌ
tab-ba-shii-ron   shii

Grass
شْ-عُشْبٌ
ô-sh-bon   sh'

Sun	Saw	Sheep

ـمسُ	مِنْـــارُ	كَبْـ
sha-m-son	mi-n-**shaa**-ron	ka-b-**shon**

Draw a line to match the words

 Brush	•	•	فُرْشَاةٌ	•	•	م ش ط
 the flame	•	•	عُشٌّ	•	•	ف ر ش ا ة
 Comb	•	•	مُشْطٌ	•	•	ع ش
 Nest	•	•	شُعْلَةٌ	•	•	ش ع ل ة

صاد Ṣād

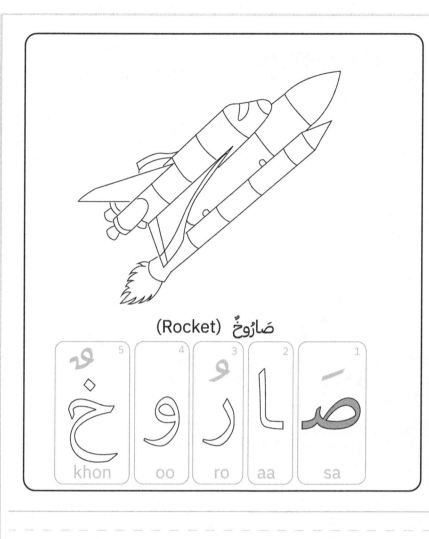

(Rocket) صَارُوخٌ

5	4	3	2	1
خ	و	ر	ا	صَ
khon	oo	ro	aa	sa

Final	Medial	Initial
ـص	ـصـ	صـ

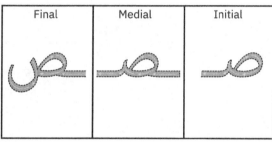

ص ص ص ص ص ص ص ص ص

صَارُوخٌ صَارُوخٌ صَارُوخٌ صَارُوخٌ

mi-qa-çon
(Scissors)

ä-ssii-ron
(Juice)

ça-h-non
(Dish)

صَحْنْ صَحْنْ	صَحْنْ 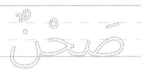

صـ ـصَحْنْ

عَصِيرٌ عَصِيرٌ 	عَصِيرٌ

ـصـ عَصِيرٌ

مِقَصٌّ مِقَصٌّ 	مِقَصٌّ

ص مِقَصٌّ

57

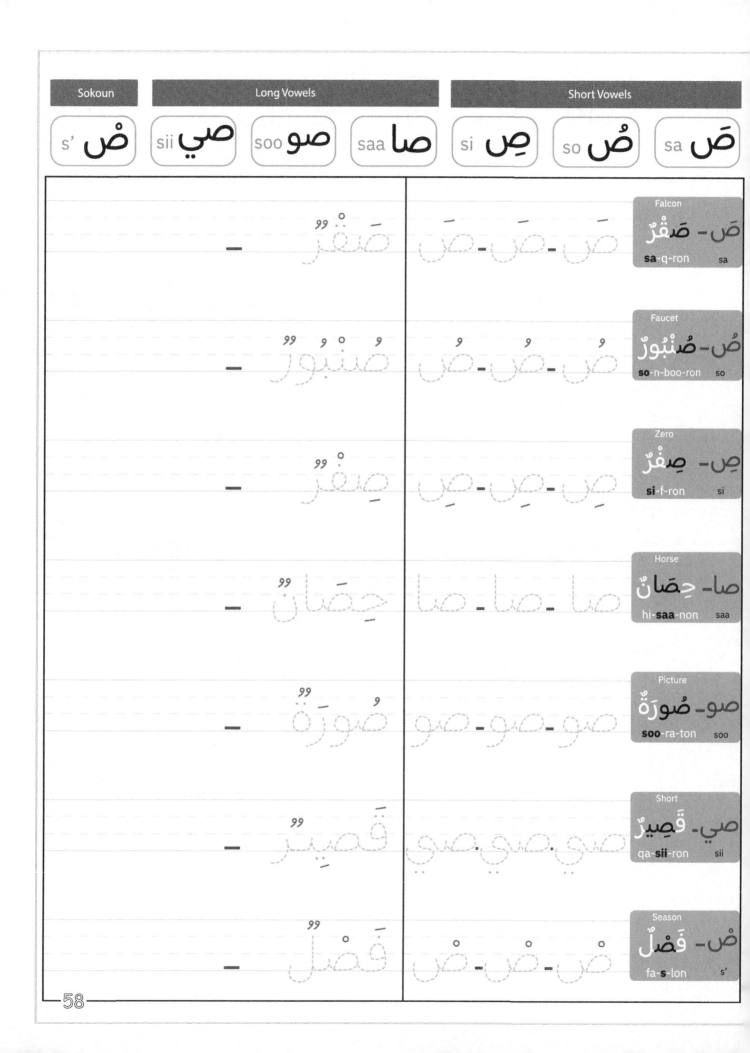

Sokoun	Long Vowels	Short Vowels

ضْ s' — صي sii — صو soo — صا saa — صِ si — صُ so — صَ sa

Falcon
صَ - صَقْرٌ
sa-q-ron   sa

Faucet
صُ - صُنْبُورٌ
so-n-boo-ron   so

Zero
صِ - صِفْرٌ
si-f-ron   si

Horse
صا - حِصَانٌ
hi-saa-non   saa

Picture
صو - صُورَةٌ
soo-ra-ton   soo

Short
صي - قَصِيرٌ
qa-sii-ron   sii

Season
ضْ - فَصْلٌ
fa-s-lon   s'

58

Cage	Castle	Whistle

قَفـ	قَـْرُ	ـفَارَةٌ
qa-fa-**son**	qa-**ss**-ron	**sa**-ffaa-ra-ton

Draw a line to match the words

Faucet		
	مِقَصٌّ	ص ق ر 
Falcon 	حِصَانٌ	ص ن ب و ر 
Scissors 	صُنْبُورٌ	ح ص ا ن
Horse 	صَقْرٌ	م ق ص

Dād ضاد

Final	Medial	Initial
ـض	ـضـ	ضـ

ضِفْدَعٌ (Frog)

4	3	2	1
عُ	دَ	فْ	ضِ
ôn	da	f	di

ضْ ضْ ضْ ضْ ضْ ضْ ضْ

ضِفْدَعٌ ضِفْدَعٌ ضِفْدَعٌ ضِفْدَعٌ ضِفْدَعٌ

da-r-son (Molar) ضَرْسٌ	kho-da-ron (Vegetables) خُضَرٌ	ba-y-don (Egg) بَيْضٌ

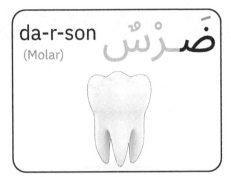

ضَ ضَرْسٌ ضَرْسٌ ضَرْسٌ

خُضَرٌ خُضَرٌ خُضَرٌ

بَيْضٌ بَيْضٌ بَيْضٌ

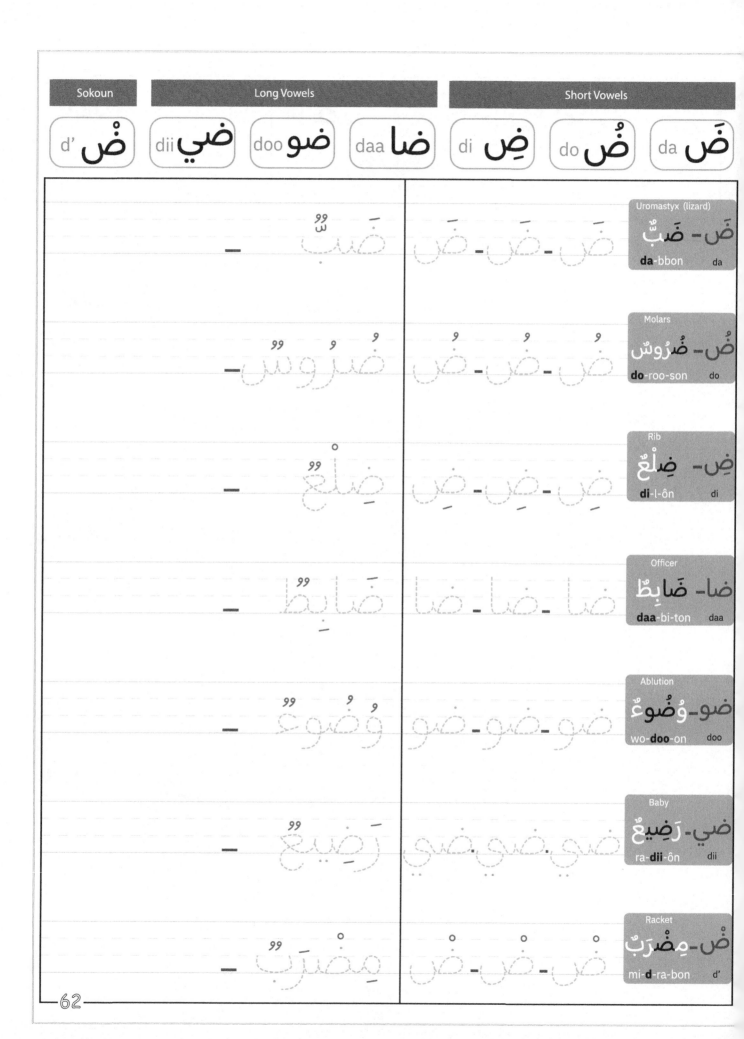

Uromastyx (lizard)
ضَ- ضَبّ
da-bbon   da

Molars
ضُ- ضُرُوسٌ
do-roo-son   do

Rib
ضِ- ضِلْعٌ
di-l-ôn   di

Officer
ضَا- ضَابِطٌ
daa-bi-ton   daa

Ablution
ضُو- وُضُوءٌ
wo-**doo**-on   doo

Baby
ضِي- رَضِيعٌ
ra-**dii**-ôn   dii

Racket
ضْ- مِضْرَبٌ
mi-**d**-ra-bon   d'

Earth	Egg	Hyena

الْأَرْ.........	بَيْ.........ةٌ	.........بْعٌ
al-ar-**d**	ba-y--**da**-ton	**da**-b-ôn

Draw a line to match the words

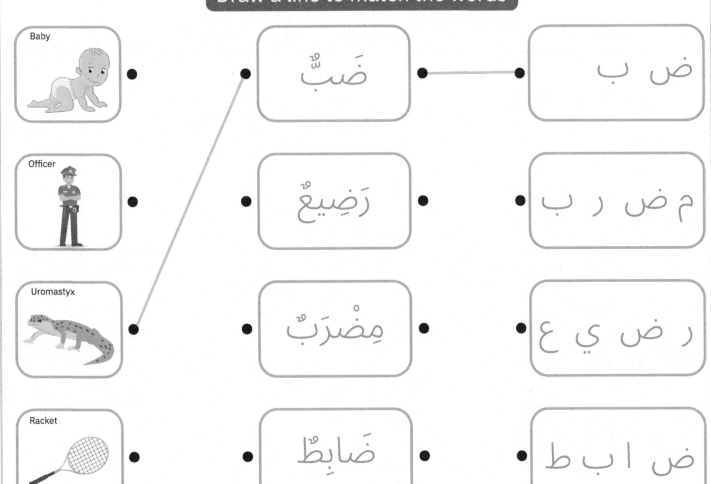

Baby		ضَبٌّ	ض ب
Officer		رَضِيعٌ	م ض ر ب
Uromastyx		مِضْرَبٌ	ر ض ي ع
Racket		ضَابِطٌ	ض ا ب ط

Tā طاء

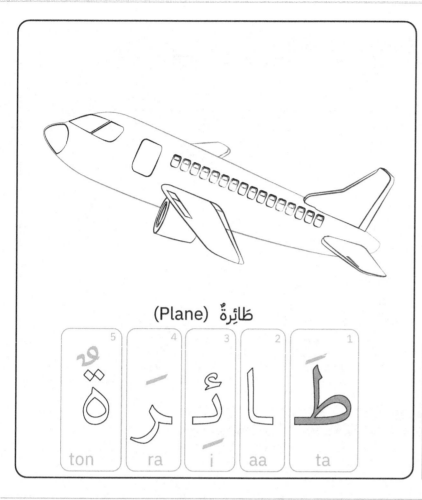

ظَائِرَةٌ (Plane)

5	4	3	2	1
ة	ـرَ	ئـ	ا	طَ
ton	ra	i	aa	ta

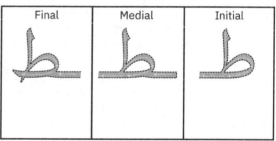

Final	Medial	Initial
ـط	ـطـ	طـ

ط ط ط ط ط ط ط ط ط ط

طَائِرَةٌ طَائِرَةٌ طَائِرَةٌ طَائِرَةٌ طَائِرَةٌ

kha-y-ton (Thread) خَيْط	ma-ta-ron (Rain) مَطَر	ta-rii-qon (Road) طَرِيق

ط | طَرِيق

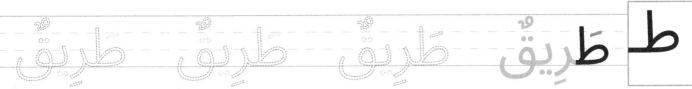

ط | مَطَر

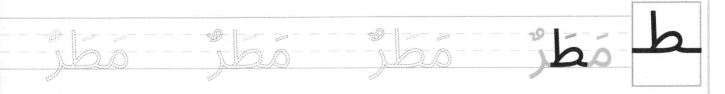

ط | خَيْط

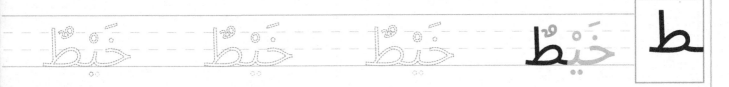

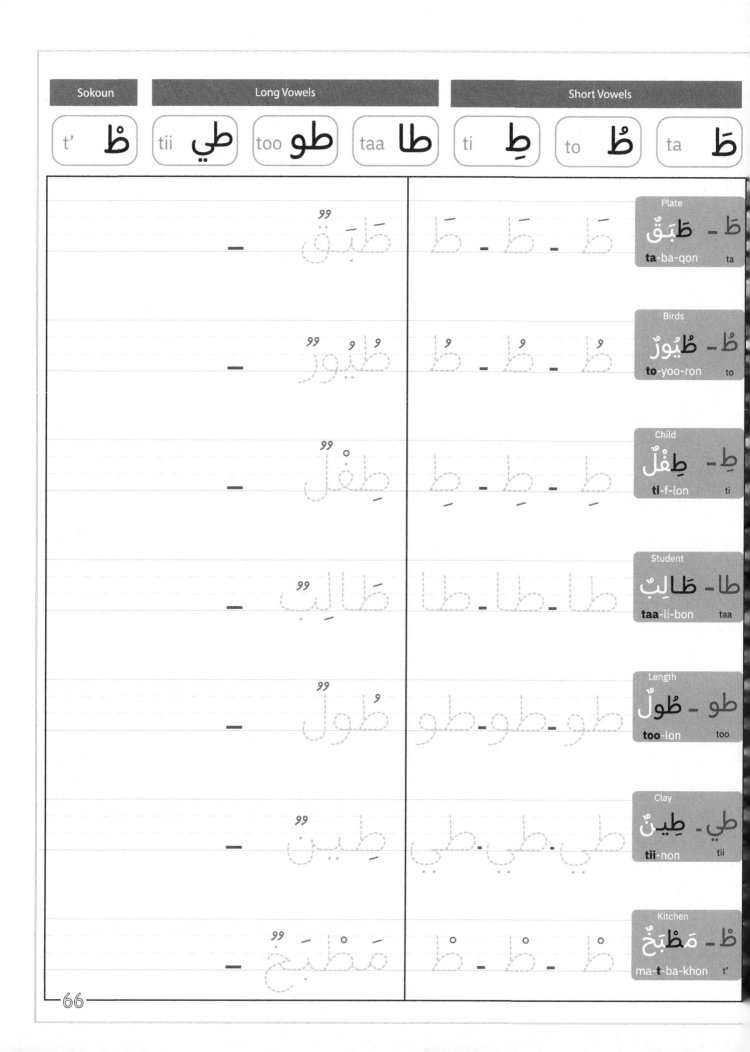

		Plate
		ظَ - طَبَقٌ
		ta-ba-qon **ta**

		Birds
		ظُ - طُيُورٌ
		to-yoo-ron **to**

		Child
		طِ - طِفْلٌ
		ti-f-lon **ti**

		Student
		طَا - طَالِبٌ
		taa-li-bon **taa**

		Length
		طُو - طُولٌ
		too-lon **too**

		Clay
		طِي - طِينٌ
		tii-non **tii**

		Kitchen
		ظْ - مَطْبَخٌ
		ma-t-ba-khon **t'**

Fill in the blank with the correct letter ط ـطـ ـط

Cat

قِـــطّ

qi-**tton**

Hammer

مِـــرْقَةٌ

mi-**t**-ra-qa-ton

Drum

ـــبْلٌ

ta-b-lon

Draw a line to match the words

Kitchen

مَطَرٌ

خ ي ط

Thread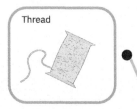

مَطْبَخٌ

م ط ر

Child

طِفْلٌ

ط ف ل

Rain

خَيْطٌ

م ط ب خ

Zhā ظاء

ظَبْيٌ (Antelope)

ظَ	بْ	يٌ
yon	b	zha

Final	Medial	Initial
ظ	ـظـ	ظـ

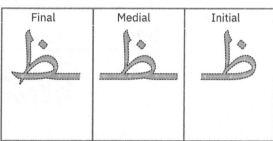

iss-tay-qa-zha
(He woke up)
إِسْتَيْقَظَ

mi-zha-lla-ton
(Umbrella)
مِظَلَّة

zho-f-ron
(Nail)
ظُفُر

ظ ظُفُر ظُفُر

ظ مِظَلَّة مِظَلَّة

ظ إِسْتَيْقَظَ إِسْتَيْقَظَ

69

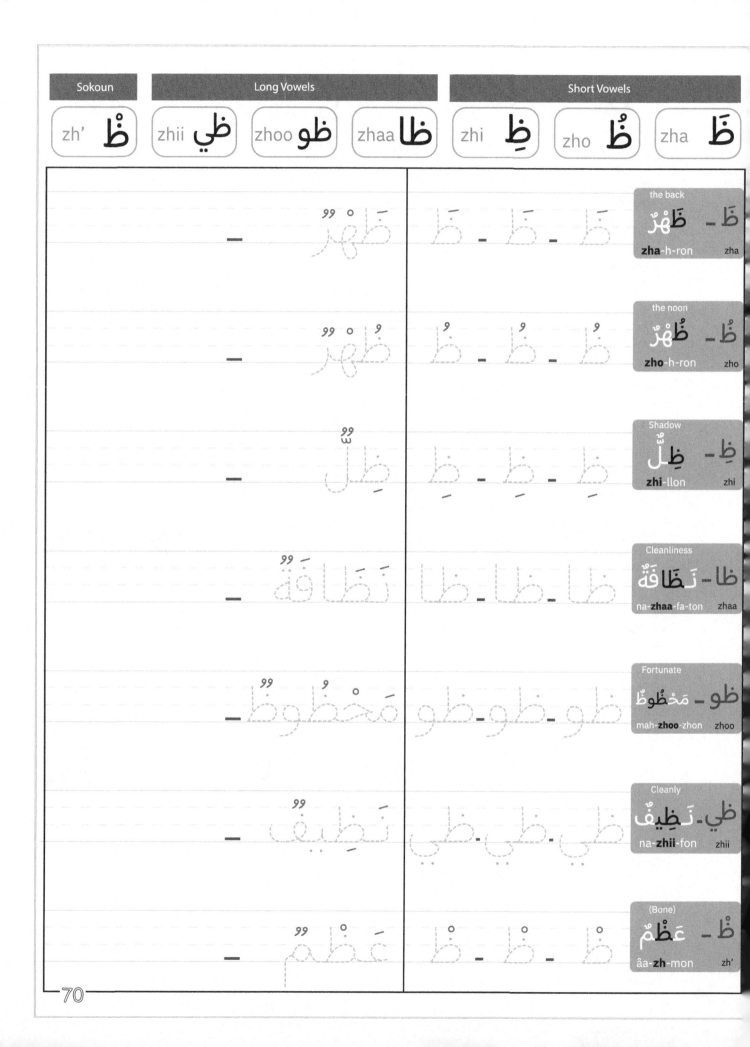

the back
ظَ ـ ظَهْرٌ
zha-h-ron   zha

the noon
ظُ ـ ظُهْرٌ
zho-h-ron   zho

Shadow
ظِ ـ ظِلّ
zhi-llon   zhi

Cleanliness
ظَا ـ نَظَافَةٌ
na-zhaa-fa-ton   zhaa

Fortunate
ظُو ـ مَحْظُوظٌ
mah-zhoo-zhon   zhoo

Cleanly
ظِي ـ نَظِيفٌ
na-zhii-fon   zhii

(Bone)
ظْ ـ عَظْمٌ
âa-zh-mon   zh'

Memorize	Glasses	Envelope

ـحِفْ	نَـَّارَاتُ	ـَرْفُ
hi-f-**zhon**	na-**zhaa**-raa-ton	**zha**-r-fon

Draw a line to match the words

the noon		
	ظُهْرُ	ظ ف ر

the back		
	ظُفْرُ	ظَ ه ر

Umbrella		
	ظُهْرُ	م ظ ل ة

Nail		
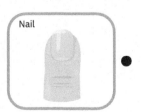	مِظَلَّةُ	ظُ ه ر

Ain

عُصْفُورٌ (Bird)

5	4	3	2	1
ron	oo	f	ss	ô

Final	Medial	Initial
ـع	ـعـ	عـ

da-bb-ôn (Hyena)	ضَبُع	älo-â-bon (Toys)	لُعَب	ây-non (Eye)	عَيْن

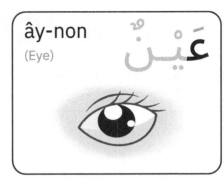

عَيْن	عَـ

عَيْنُ عَيْنُ عَيْنُ عَيْنُ عَيْنُ

لُعَب	عـ

لُعَبُ لُعَبُ لُعَبُ لُعَبُ لُعَبُ

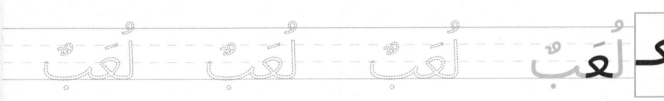

ضَبُع	ع

ضَبُعْ ضَبُعْ ضَبُعْ ضَبُعْ ضَبُعْ

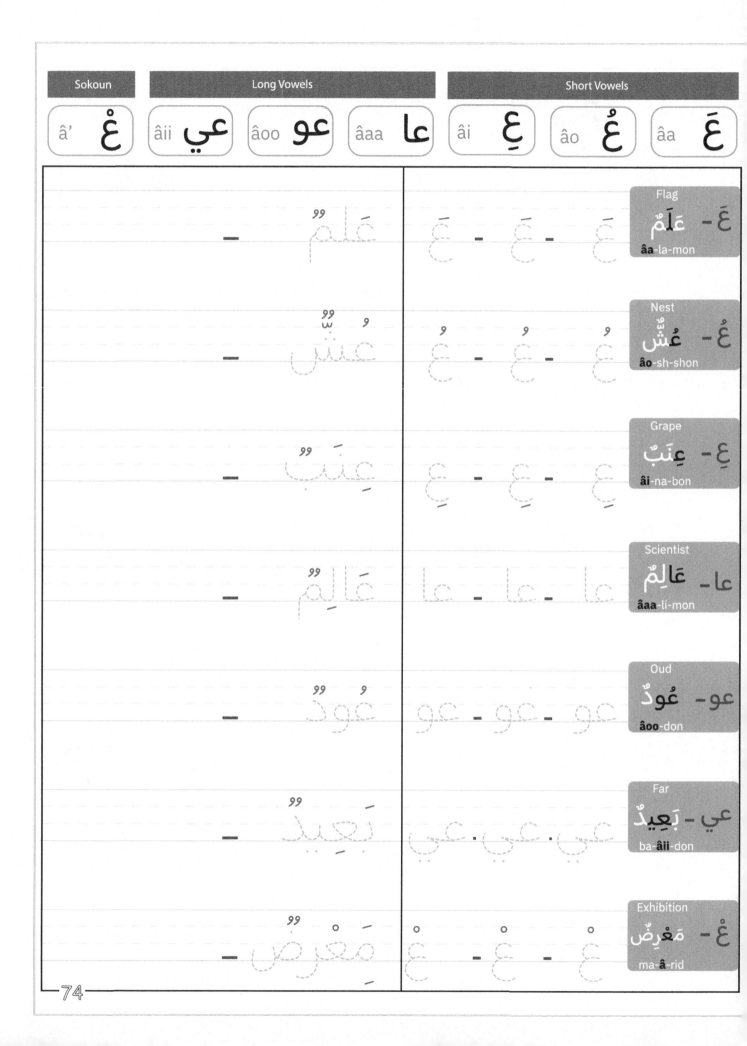

Flag
عَ - عَلَمٌ
âa-la-mon

Nest
عُ - عُشٌّ
âo-sh-shon

Grape
عِ - عِنَبٌ
âi-na-bon

Scientist
عا - عَالِمٌ
âaa-li-mon

Oud
عو - عُودٌ
âoo-don

Far
عي - بَعِيدٌ
ba-**âii**-don

Exhibition
غْ - مَعْرِضٌ
ma-**â**-rid

74

Fill in the blank with the correct letter

Square	Fox	Wheel

مُرَبَّ ـــُ

mo-ra-bba-**âon**

ثَ ـــُ لَبُ

tha-**â**-la-bon

عَجَلَةٌ

âa-ja-la-ton

Draw a line to match the words

Hyena

عِنَبٌ

ل ع ب

Grape

عَيْنٌ

ض ب ع

Eye

لُعَبٌ

ع ي ن

Toys

ضَبْعٌ

ع ن ب

75

Ghain غين

(Crow) غُرَاب

4	3	2	1
بـ	ا ـر	ـرَ	غُ
bon	aa	ra	gho

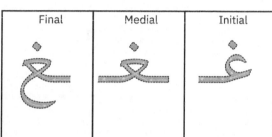

Final	Medial	Initial
ـغ	ـغـ	غـ

غ غ غ غ غ غ غ غ غ غ

غُرَاب غُرَاب غُرَاب غُرَاب غُرَاب غُرَاب

sa-m-ghon (Glue)	صَمْغ	mi-gh-sa-lon (Washbasin)	مِغْسَل	gho-ss-non (Branch)	غُصْن

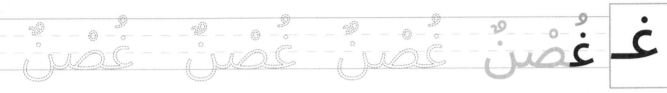

غـ غُصْن غُصْن غُصْن غُصْن غُصْن

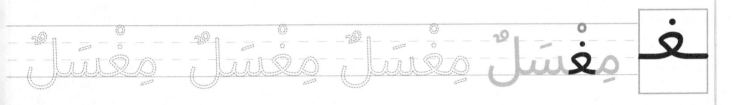

ـغـ مِغْسَل مِغْسَل مِغْسَل مِغْسَل

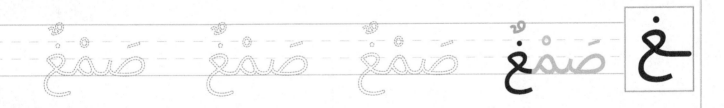

ـغ صَمْغ صَمْغ صَمْغ صَمْغ

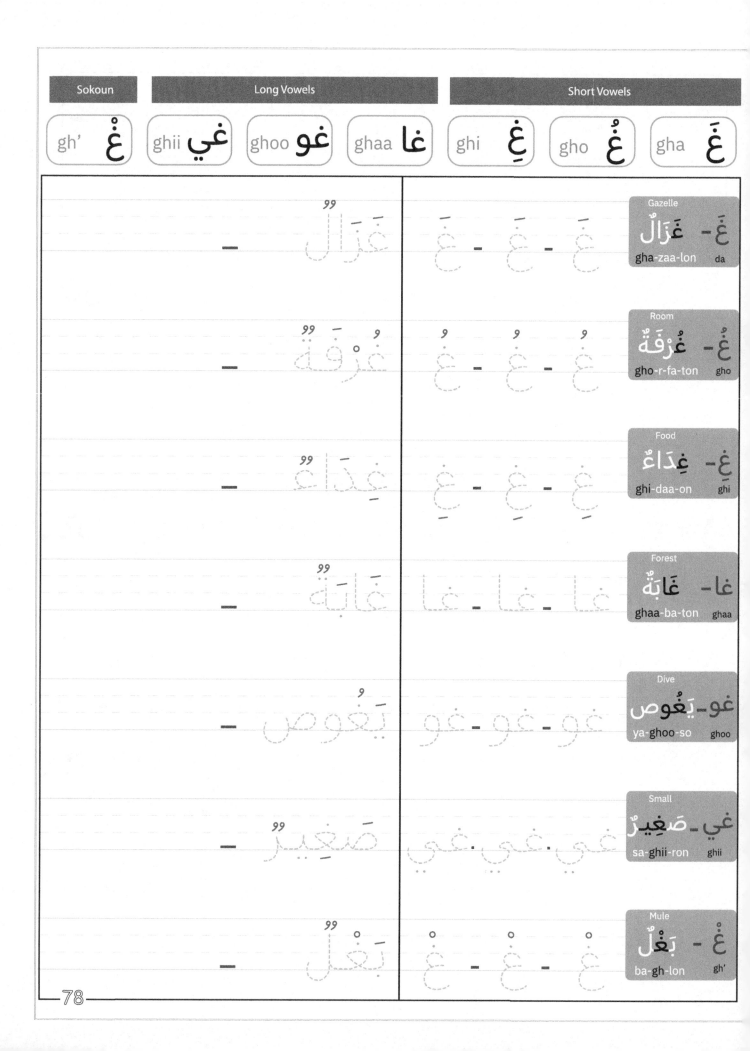

	Gazelle
	غَـ - غَزَالٌ
	gha-zaa-lon da

	Room
	غُـ - غُرْفَةٌ
	gho-r-fa-ton gho

	Food
	غِـ - غِذَاءٌ
	ghi-daa-on ghi

	Forest
	غَا - غَابَةٌ
	ghaa-ba-ton ghaa

	Dive
	غو - يَغُوصُ
	ya-ghoo-so ghoo

	Small
	غي - صَغِيرٌ
	sa-ghii-ron ghii

	Mule
	غْ - بَغْلٌ
	ba-gh-lon gh'

Complète chaque mot avec la lettre appropriée   غ ـ ـغـ ـغ

Brain	Parrot	Submarine
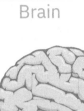		
دمَا........	بَبْـ........ـاءُ	........ـوَّاصَةٌ
di-maa-**ghon**	ba-b-**ghaa**-on	**gha**-wwaa-sa-ton

Draw a line to match the words

Gazelle

Mule

Branch

Washbasin

بَغْلٌ

مِغْسَلٌ

غَزَالٌ

غُصْنٌ

غ ز ا ل

غ ص ن

ب غ ل

م غ س ل

79

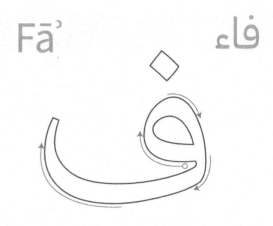

فاء Fāʾ

فِيلٌ (Elephant)

lon	ii	fi

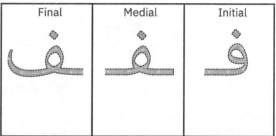

Final	Medial	Initial
ف	ـفـ	فـ

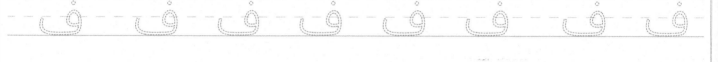

mi-â-ta-fon	qa-fa-son	fol-fo-lon
(Coat) مِعْطَف	(Cage) قَفَص	(Pepper) فُلْفُل

	ف
فُلْفُل فُلْفُل	ـف

 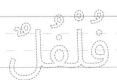 

	ف
قَفَص قَفَص	قَفَص ـف

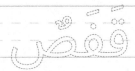 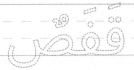 

	ف
مِعْطَف مِعْطَف	مِعْطَف ـف

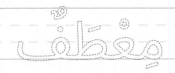  

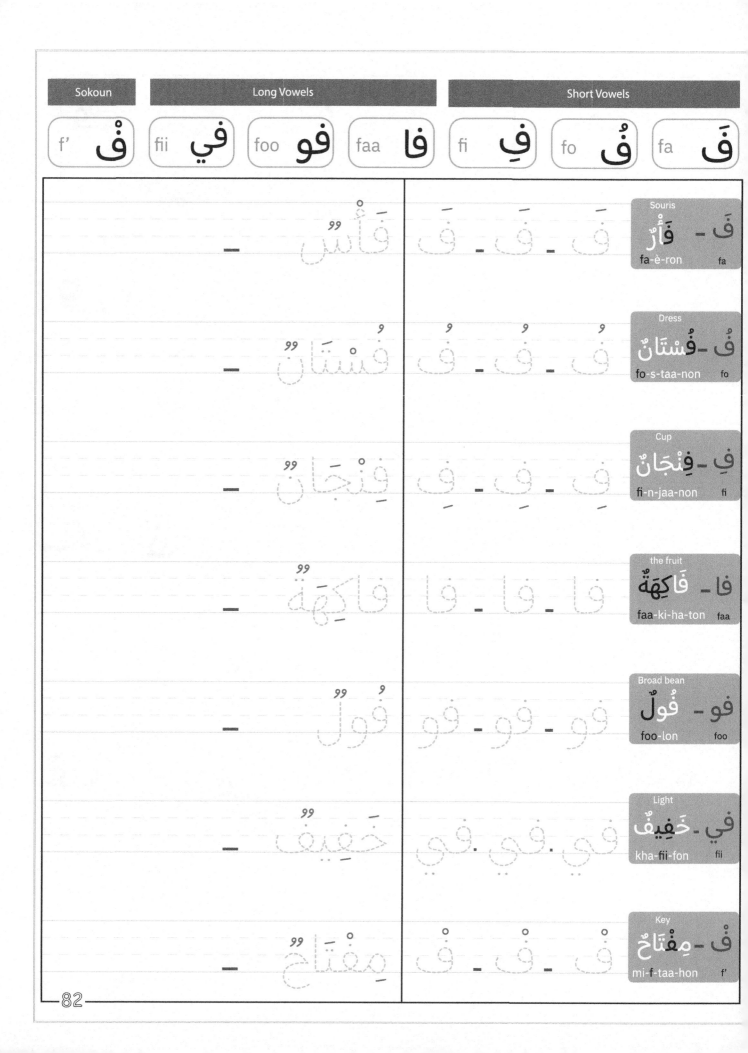

Sokoun	Long Vowels			Short Vowels		
f' ـفْ	fii فِي	foo فُو	faa فَا	fi فِ	fo فُ	fa فَ

Souris — فَ - فَأْرٌ — fa-è-ron — fa

Dress — فُ - فُسْتَانٌ — fo-s-taa-non — fo

Cup — فِ - فِنْجَانٌ — fi-n-jaa-non — fi

the fruit — فَا - فَاكِهَةٌ — faa-ki-ha-ton — faa

Broad bean — فُو - فُولٌ — foo-lon — foo

Light — فِي - خَفِيفٌ — kha-fii-fon — fii

Key — فْ - مِفْتَاحٌ — mi-f-taa-hon — f'

82

Fill in the blank with the correct letter ف ـ ف ـ فـ

Half	Window	Butterfly

نِصْفٌ	نَافِذَةٌ	فَرَاشَةٌ
ni-ss-**fon**	naa-**fi**-dha-ton	**fa**-raa-sha-ton

Draw a line to match the words

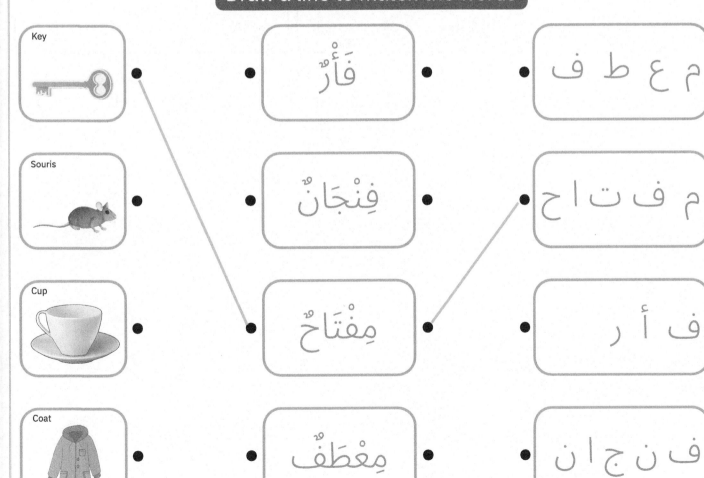

Key

Souris

Cup

Coat

فَأْرٌ

فِنْجَانٌ

مِفْتَاحٌ

مِعْطَفٌ

م ع ط ف

م ف ت ا ح

ف أ ر

ف ن ج ان

قاف Qāf

قَمِيصٌ (Shirt)

4	3	2	1
ص	يـ	ـمـ	قَ
son	ii	mi	qa

Final	Medial	Initial
ق	ـقـ	قـ

ص ص ص ص ص ص ص ص ص ص

قَمِيضٌ قَمِيضٌ قَمِيضٌ قَمِيضٌ قَمِيضٌ

na_fa_qon
(Tunnel)

نَفَقٌ

ha-qii-ba-ton
(Suitcase)

حَقِيبَةٌ

qa-ma-ron
(Moon)

قَمَرٌ

قـ

قَمَرٌ

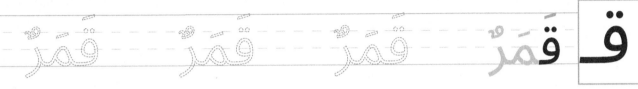

ـقـ

حَقِيبَةٌ

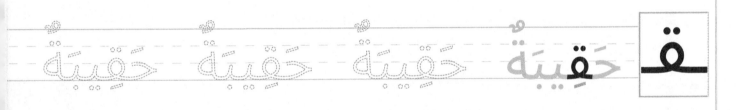

ـق

نَفَقٌ

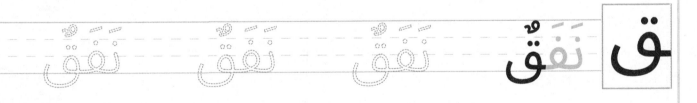

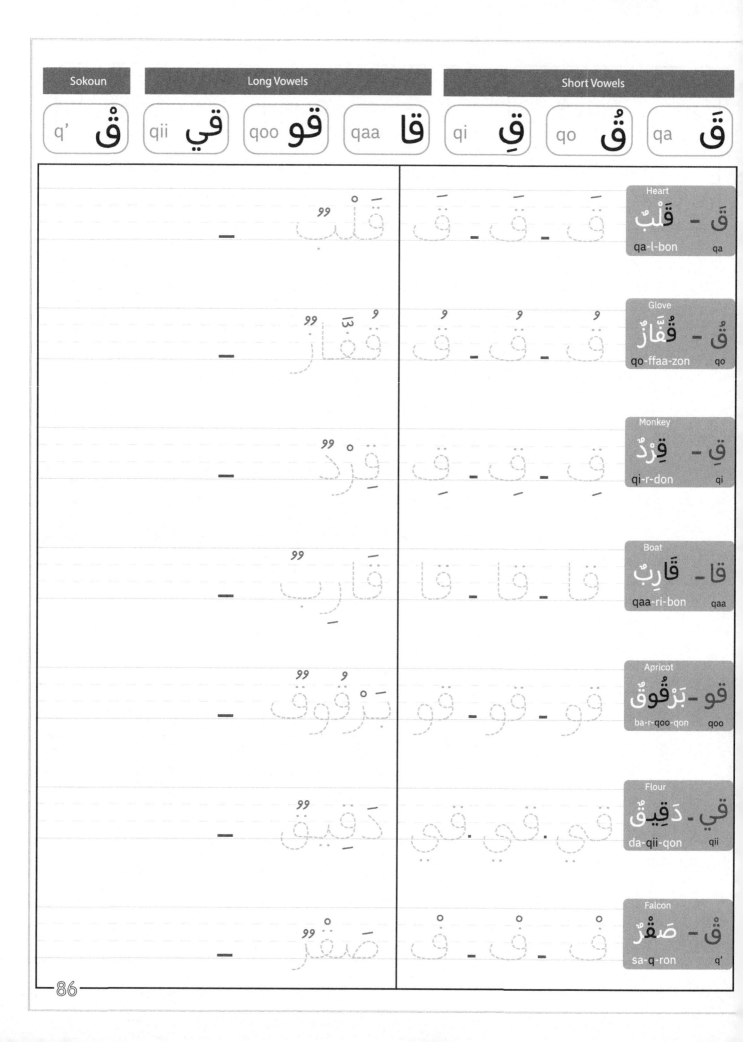

Heart
قَ - قَلْب
qa-l-bon — qa

Glove
قُ - قُفَّازٌ
qo-ffaa-zon — qo

Monkey
قِ - قِرْدٌ
qi-r-don — qi

Boat
قا - قَارِبٌ
qaa-ri-bon — qaa

Apricot
قو - بَرْقُوقٌ
ba-r-qoo-qon — qoo

Flour
قي - دَقِيقٌ
da-qii-qon — qii

Falcon
قْ - صَقْرٌ
sa-q-ron — q'

Barber	Scissors	Train

ـــــ حَلَّاقُ	مِـــــصّ	طَارُ ـــــ
ha-llaa-**qon**	mi-**qa**-sson	**qi**-taa-ron

Draw a line to match the words

Boat 	قُفَازٌ	ق ر د
Glove	قِرْدٌ	ق ف ا ز
Monkey 	حَقِيبَةٌ	ق ا ر ب
Suitcase	قَارِبٌ	ح ق ي ب ة

كاف Kāf

كِتَابٌ (Book)

4	3	2	1
ب	ا تَ	كِ	
bon	aa	ta	ki

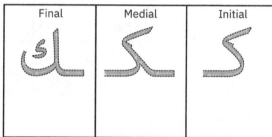

Final	Medial	Initial
ك	ك	ك

ك ك ك ك ك ك ك ك ك ك

كِتَابْ كِتَابْ كِتَابْ كِتَابْ كِتَابْ كِتَابْ كِتَابْ

sa-ma-kon
(Fish)
سَمَك

ma-k-ta-bon
(Desk)
مَكْتَب

ka-â-kon
(Cake)
كَعْك

ك	كَعْك كَعْك كَعْك كَعْك كَعْك

ك	مَكْتَب مَكْتَب مَكْتَب مَكْتَب مَكْتَب

ك	سَمَك سَمَك سَمَك سَمَك سَمَك

| k' كْ | kii كي | koo كو | kaa كا | ki كِ | ko كُ | ka كَ |

Dog
كَ - كَلْب
ka-l-bon | ka

Chair
كُ - كُرْسِيٌّ
ko-r-si-yon | ko

Book
كِ - كِتَاب
ki-taa-bon | ki

Writer
كَا - كَاتِب
kaa-ti-bon | kaa

Cup
كو - كُوب
koo-bon | koo

Bag
كي - كِيسٌّ
kii-son | kii

Idea
كْ - فِكْرَة
fi-k-ra-ton | k'

Fill in the blank with the correct letter ك ـك ـكـ

Rooster

دِيـ......ُ

dii-**kon**

Chick

كَتـ......ُوت

qa-t-**koo**-ton

Ball

......ُرَةٌ

ko-ra-ton

Draw a line to match the words

Bag

Dog

Chair

Cake

كِيسٌ

كَعْكٌ

كُرْسِيٌّ

كَلْبٌ

ك ل ب

ك ر س ي

ك ع ك

ك ي س

Lām

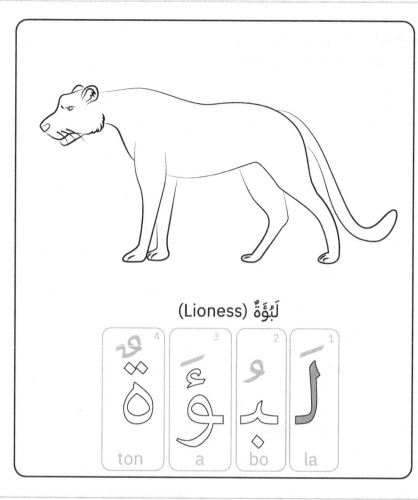

لَبُؤَةٌ (Lioness)

4	3	2	1
ؤ ة	ءو	بٔ	أَ
ton	a	bo	la

Final	Medial	Initial
ـل	ـلـ	لـ

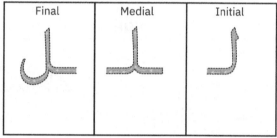

ل ل ل ل ل ل ل ل ل ل ل ل ل ل

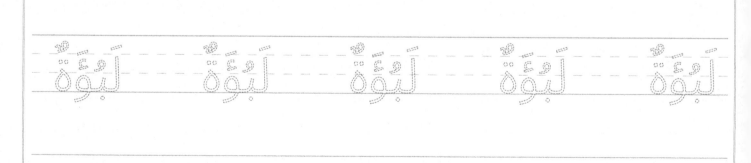

لَبُؤَةٌ لَبُؤَةٌ لَبُؤَةٌ لَبُؤَةٌ لَبُؤَةٌ لَبُؤَةٌ لَبُؤَةٌ

ba-sa-lon	qa-l-bon	lih-h-ya-ton
(Onion) بَصَل	(Heart) قَلْب	(Beard) لِحْيَة

لِحْيَة

  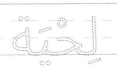 

قَلْب

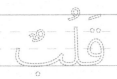 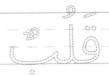 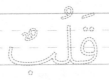 

بَصَل

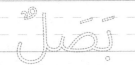   

93

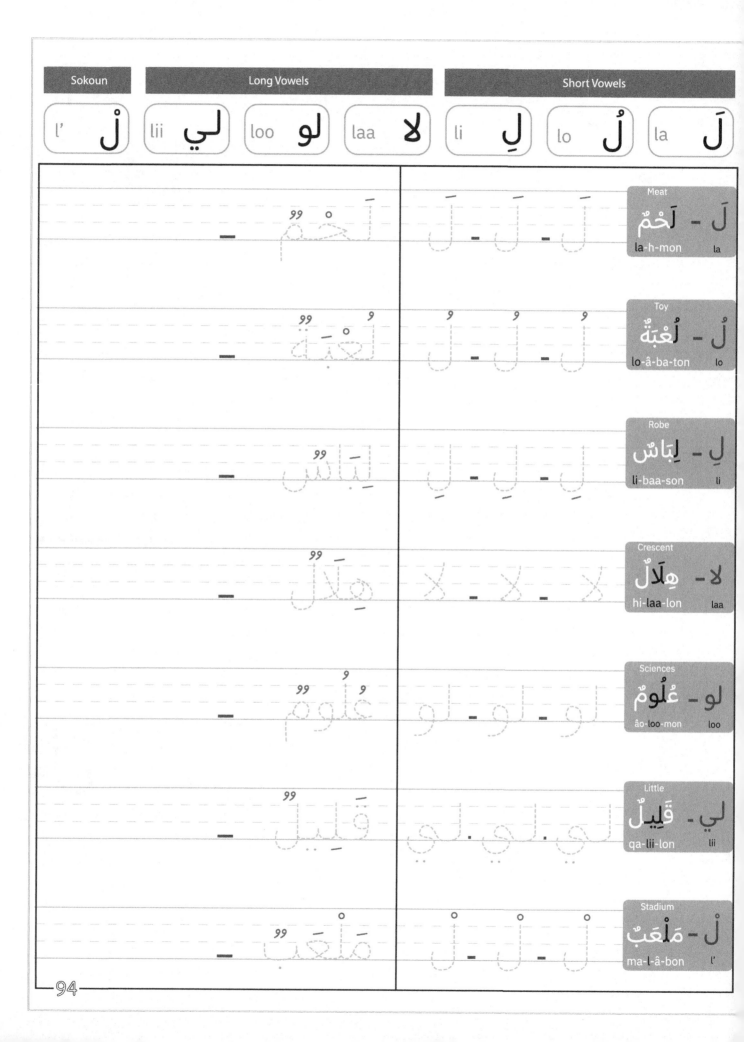

		Meat
		لَ - لَحْمٌ
		la-h-mon / la

		Toy
		لُ - لُعْبَةٌ
		lo-â-ba-ton / lo

		Robe
		لِ - لِبَاسٌ
		li-baa-son / li

		Crescent
		لا - هِلَالٌ
		hi-laa-lon / laa

		Sciences
		لو - عُلُومٌ
		âo-loo-mon / loo

		Little
		لِي - قَلِيلٌ
		qa-lii-lon / lii

		Stadium
		لْ - مَلْعَبٌ
		ma-l-â-bon / l'

Camel	Bus	Tongue
		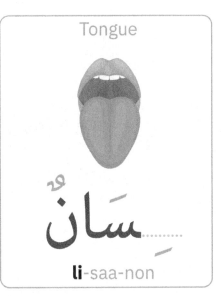
جَمـ.........	حَافِـ......ة	.........ـسَانٌ
ja-ma-**lon**	haa-fi-**la**-ton	**li**-saa-non

Draw a line to match the words

Stadium 	هِلَالٌ	م ل ع ب
Crescent 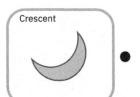	بَصَلٌ	ل ح ي ة
Beard 	مَلْعَبٌ	ب ص ل
Onion 	لِحْيَةٌ	ﻩ ل ا ل

Mīm   ميم

(Mosque) مَسْجِدٌ

4	3	2	1
don	ji	ss	ma

Final	Medial	Initial
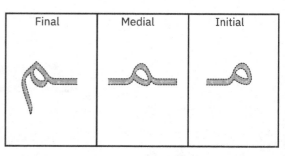		

م   م   م   م   م   م   م   م   م   م

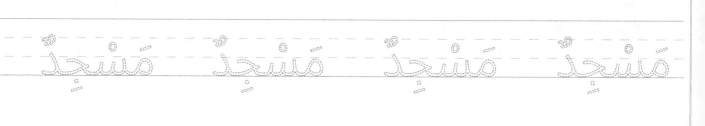

qa-la-mon
(Pencil)

hi-maa-ron
(Donkey)

ma-w-zon
(Bananas)

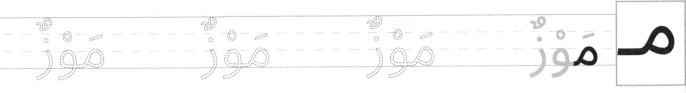

مَوْزٌ

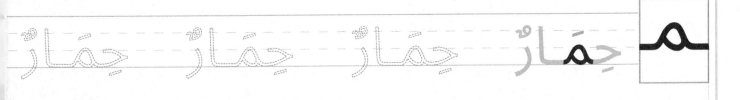

حِمَارٌ

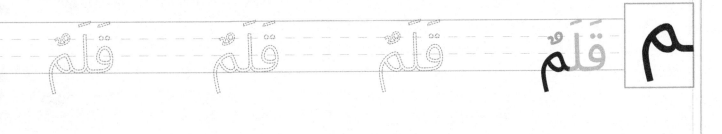

قَلَمٌ

97

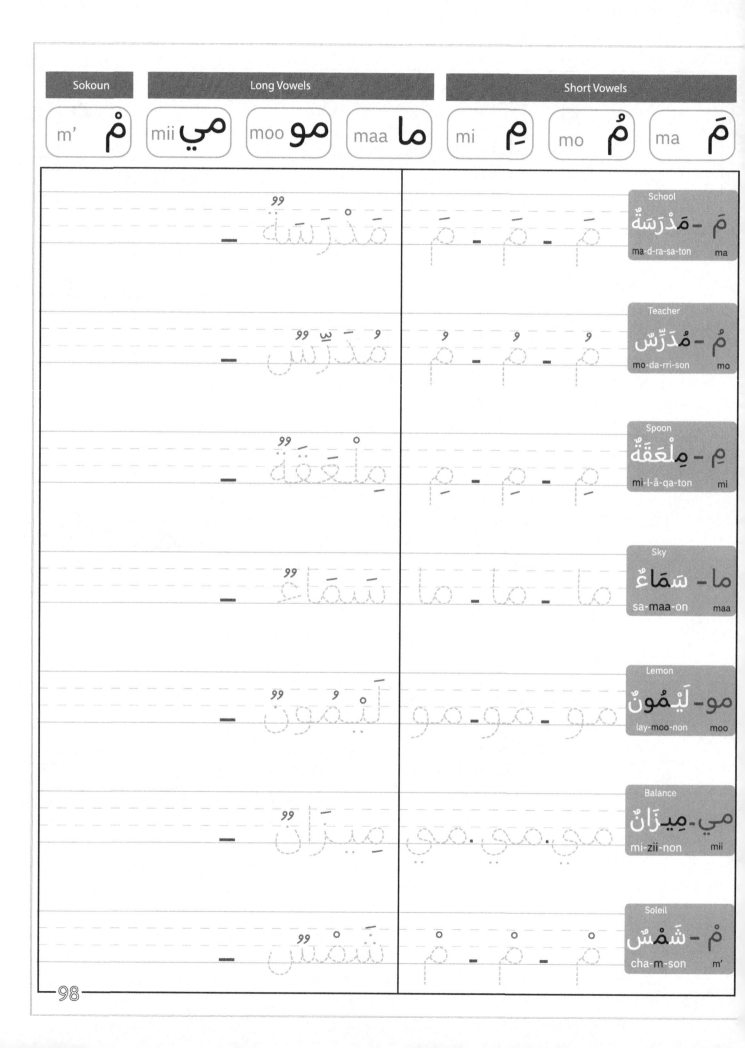

Sokoun	Long Vowels			Short Vowels		
م m'	مي mii	مو moo	ما maa	مِ mi	مُ mo	مَ ma

School
مَ - مَدْرَسَةٌ
ma-d-ra-sa-ton — ma

Teacher
مُ - مُدَرِّسٌ
mo-da-rri-son — mo

Spoon
مِ - مِلْعَقَةٌ
mi-l-â-qa-ton — mi

Sky
ما - سَمَاءٌ
sa-maa-on — maa

Lemon
مو - لَيْمُونٌ
lay-moo-non — moo

Balance
مي - مِيزَانٌ
mi-zii-non — mii

Soleil
مْ - شَمْسٌ
cha-m-son — m'

98

Fill in the blank with the correct letter

Flag	Fish	Office

عَلَ ـُ	سَ ـَكَةُ	ـَكْتَبُ
âa-la-**mon**	sa-**ma**-ka-ton	**ma**-k-ta-bon

Draw a line to match the words

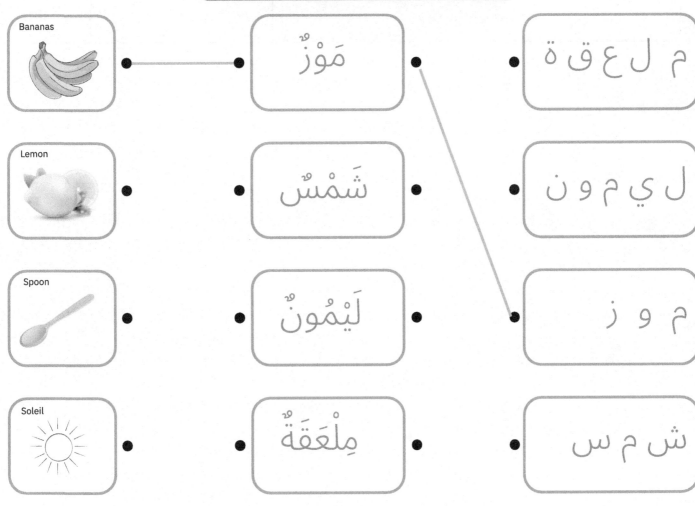

Bananas	مَوْزُ	م ل ع ق ة
Lemon	شَمْسُ	ل ي م و ن
Spoon	لَيْمُونُ	م و ز
Soleil	مِلْعَقَةُ	ش م س

Nūn

نون

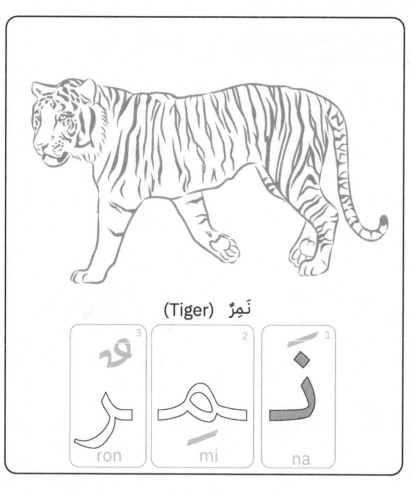

نَمِرٌ (Tiger)

Final	Medial	Initial
ن	ـنـ	نـ

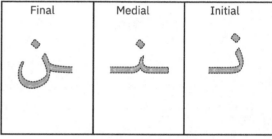

ن ن ن ن ن ن ن ن

نَمِرْ نَمِرْ نَمِرْ نَمِرْ نَمِرْ

tii-non (Fig)	تِيـن	ma-n-zi-lon (House)	مَنْزِل	na-äa-ma-ton (Ostrich)	نَعَامَة

ذ نَعَامَة نَعَامَة نَعَامَة نَعَامَة نَعَامَة نَعَامَة

نـ مَنْزِل مَنْزِل مَنْزِل مَنْزِل مَنْزِل مَنْزِل

ن تِيـن تِيـن تِيـن تِيـن تِيـن

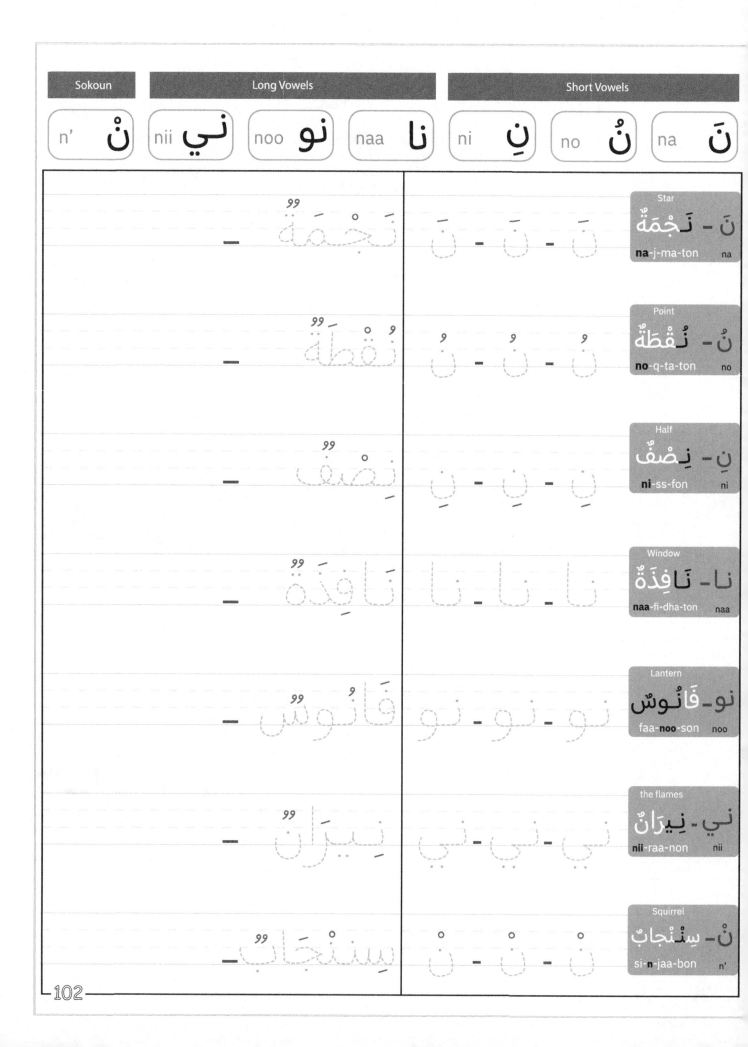

Sokoun	Long Vowels			Short Vowels		
نْ n'	نِي nii	نو noo	نا naa	نِ ni	نُ no	نَ na

Star
نَ - نَجْمَةٌ
na-j-ma-ton   na

Point
نُ - نُقْطَةٌ
no-q-ta-ton   no

Half
نِ - نِصْفٌ
ni-ss-fon   ni

Window
نا - نَافِذَةٌ
naa-fi-dha-ton   naa

Lantern
نو - فَانُوسٌ
faa-**noo**-son   noo

the flames
نِي - نِيرَانٌ
nii-raa-non   nii

Squirrel
نْ - سِنْجَابٌ
si-**n**-jaa-bon   n'

102

Balance	Grape	Ant

مِيزَا ُ	عِـ ـبُ	ـمْلَةٌ
mii-zaa-**non**	âi-**na**-bon	**na**-m-la-ton

Draw a line to match the words

 Lantern — نَجْمَةٌ — ن ع ا م ة

 Star — فَانُوسٌ — ن ا ف ذ ة

 Window — نَعَامَةٌ — ن ج م ة

 Ostrich — نَافِذَةٌ — ف ا ن و س

Hā

هاء

هَدِيَّةٌ (Gift)

4	3	2	1
ةٌ	يَّ	دِ	هَ
ton	yya	di	ha

Final	Medial	Initial
ـه	ـهـ	هـ

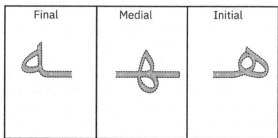

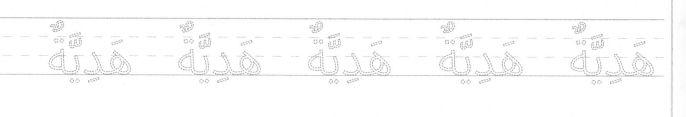

mo-na-bbi-hon (Alarm clock) مُنَبِّهٌ	sa-h-mo n (Arrow) سَهْمٌ	ha-ra-mon (Pyramid) هَرَمٌ

  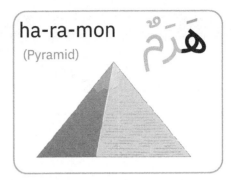

    هَرَمٌ هـ

   سَهْمٌ ط

   مُنَبِّهٌ ﻪ

| h' ثْ | hii هي | hoo هو | haa ها | hi هِ | ho هُ | ha هَ |

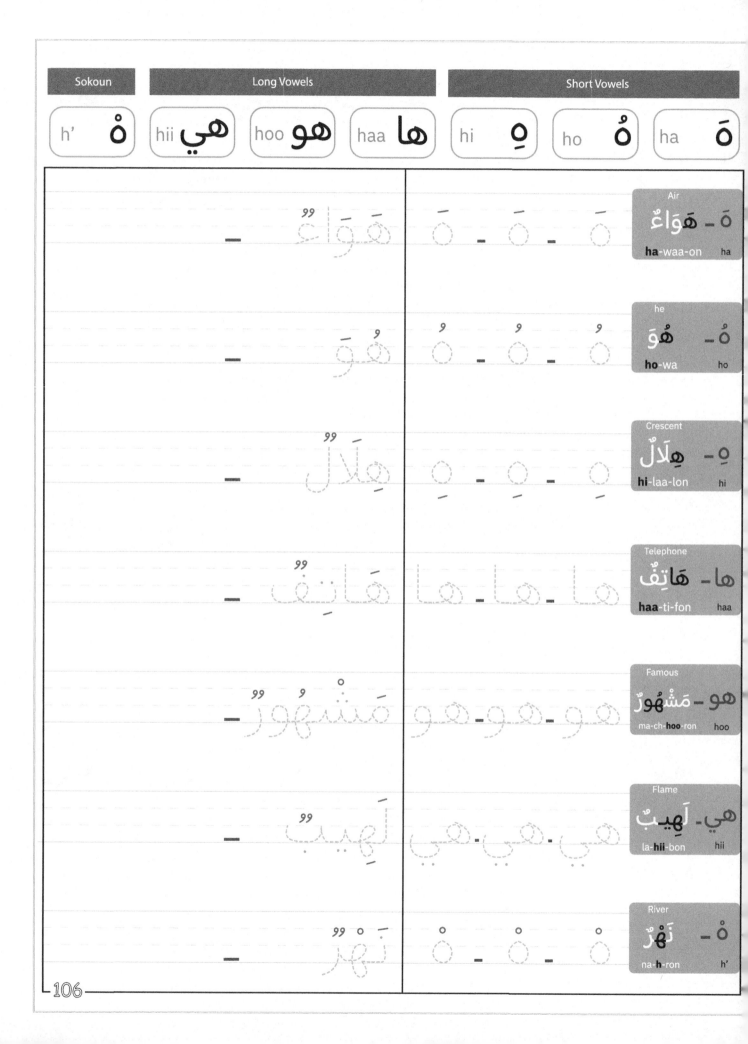

Air
 هَوَاءٌ - هَ
ha-waa-on — ha

he
هُوَ - هُ
ho-wa — ho

Crescent
هِلَالٌ - هِ
hi-laa-lon — hi

Telephone
هَاتِفٌ - هَا
haa-ti-fon — haa

Famous
مَشْهُورٌ - هُو
ma-ch-**hoo**-ron — hoo

Flame
لَهِيبٌ - هِي
la-**hii**-bon — hii

River
نَهْرٌ - هْ
na-h-ron — h'

Fill in the blank with the correct letter

Face	Leopard	Hoopoe

وَجْ......ٌ	فَ......دٌ	......ذُهُدٌ
wa-j-**hon**	fa-**h**-don	**ho**-d-ho-don

Draw a line to match the words

Telephone

Alarm clock

Flame

Pyramid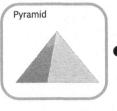

هَرَمٌ

هَاتِفٌ

مُنَبّهٌ

لَهِيبٌ

ل ه ي ب

ه ر م

م ن ب ه

ه ا ت ف

Wāw واو

(A rose) وَرْدَةٌ

ةٌ	دَ	رْ	وَ
ton	da	r	wa

Final	Medial	Initial
و	ـو	و

و و و و و و و و

وَرْدَةٌ وَرْدَةٌ وَرْدَةٌ وَرْدَةٌ وَرْدَةٌ

| | da-l-won
(Bucket) |  دَلْوٌ | la-w-zon
(Almonds) |  لَوْزٌ | wa-j-hon
(Face) |  وَجْهٌ |

وَجْهٌ   وَجْهٌ   وَجْهٌ   وَجْهٌ   **و**

لَوْزٌ   لَوْزٌ   لَوْزٌ   لَوْزٌ   **و**

دَلْوٌ   دَلْوٌ   دَلْوٌ   دَلْوٌ   **و**

		Boy وَ - وَلَدٌ **wa**-la-don wa
		Roses وُ - وُرُودٌ **wo**-roo-don wo
		A pot وِ - وِعَاءٌ **wi**-âa-on wi
		Valley وا - وَادٍ **waa**-don waa
		Peacock وو - طَاوُوسٌ taa-**woo**-son woo
		Long وي - طَوِيلٌ ta-**wii**-lon wii
		Voice وْ - صَوْتٌ sa-**w**-ton w'

Fill in the blank with the correct letter و - ﻮ - و

Puppy	Bananas	One
		1
جَرْ.........ٌ	مَ.........ْزٌ	.........َاحِدٌ
ja-r-**won**	ma-**w**-zon	**waa**-hi-don

Draw a line to match the words

Bucket

طَاوُوسٌ

و ر و د

Almonds

وُرُودٌ

ل و ز

Roses

دَلْوٌ

ط ا و و س

Peacock

لَوْزٌ

د ل و

111

ياء

Yā

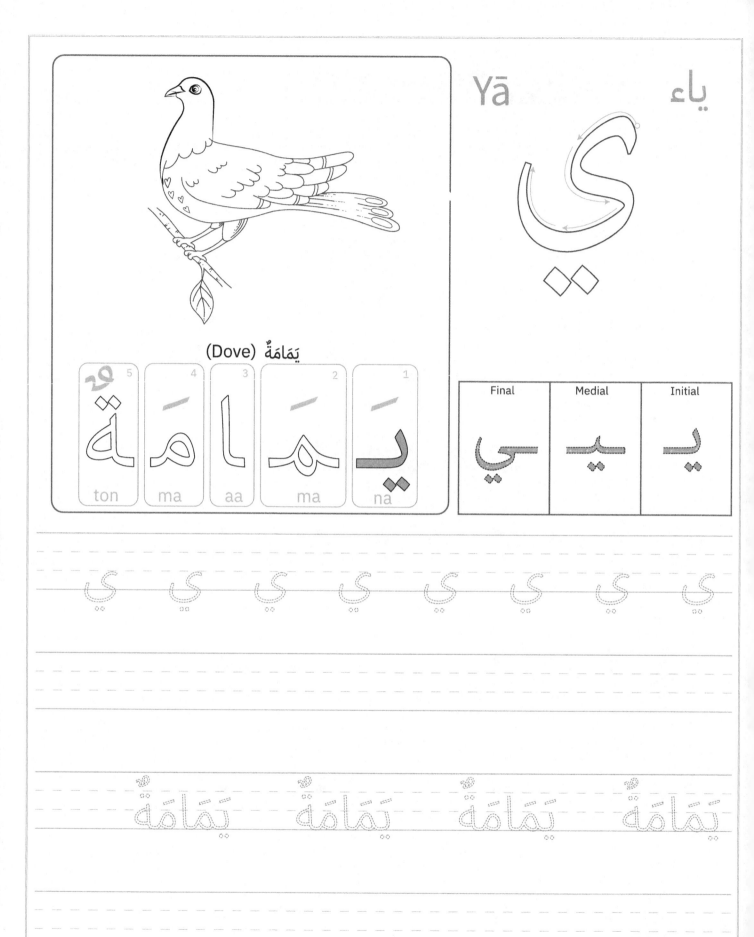

يَمَامَةٌ (Dove)

Final	Medial	Initial
ي	ـيـ	يـ

112

| sa-bi-yyon
(Boy) صَبِيٌّ  | ba-y-ton
(House) بَيْتٌ  | ya-don
(Hand) يَدٌ  |

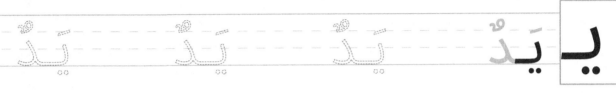

يَدٌ

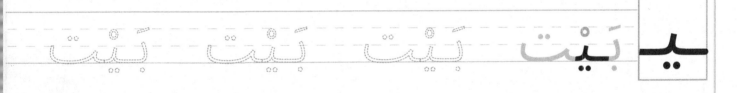

بَيْتٌ

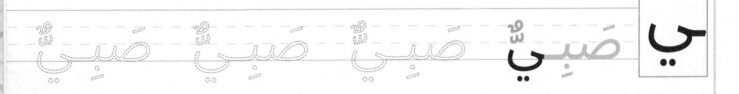

صَبِيٌّ

			Day يَ - يَوْمٌ **ya**-w-mon — ya
			he colors يُ - يُلَوِّنُ **yo**-la-wwi-no — yo
			Yen (Japan's currency) يِ - يِن **yi**-n — yi
			Jasmin يَا- يَاسِمِين **yaa**-sa-miin — yaa
			Birds يُو - طُيُورٌ to-**yoo**-ron — yoo
			My opinion يِي - رَأْيِي ra-è-**yii** — yii
			an egg يْ - بَيْضَةٌ ba-**y**-da-ton — y'

Chair

كُرْسِ.........

ko-r-si-**yon**

House

بَ.ْتٌ

ba-**y**-ton

Dragonfly

.........عْسُوبٌ

ya-â-soo-bon

Draw a line to match the words

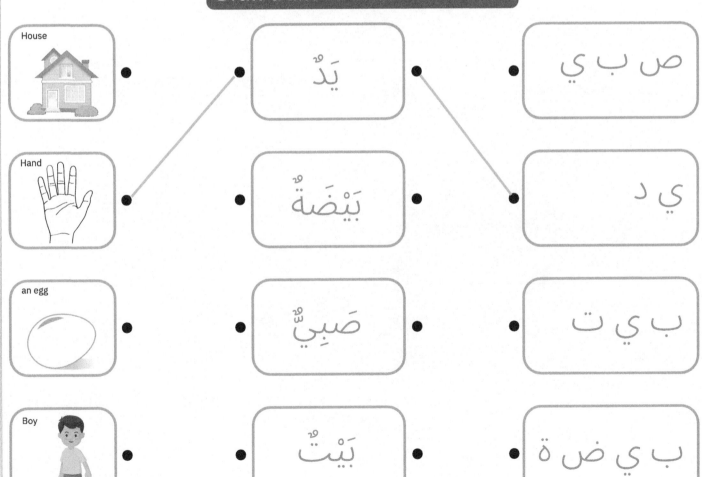

House

Hand

an egg

Boy

يَدٌ

بَيْضَةٌ

صَبِيٌّ

بَيْتٌ

ص ب ي

ي د

ب ي ت

ب ي ض ة

Made in the USA
Las Vegas, NV
15 January 2024

84425046R00070